# MASTERING CENSUS & MILITARY RECORDS

Volume III of *Quillen's Essentials of Genealogy*
3rd Edition

www.essentialgenealogy.com

## PRAISE FOR DAN'S GENEALOGY BOOKS

"W. Daniel Quillen's *Secrets of Tracing Your Ancestors* shows those new to the hobby how to begin their genealogy, while showing seasoned family historians some new tricks. Covering the basics such as organization, the best genealogical websites and how to do family group sheets, Quillen approaches his subject with passion and a touch of humor. The book also looks at features of advanced genealogy such as using professionals and writing your personal history. Most chapters feature additional resources pointing readers toward other resources." – *Family Chronicle magazine*

"Your book *Secrets of Tracing your Ancestors* has been extremely helpful to me in a renewal of my genealogy interests." – *Nancy Dailey*

"I would like to thank you for writing a very informative book. There was a lot of information that I did not know about…" – *Donna Perryman Moon*

"I purchased your book and have found it most helpful." – *Glenda Laney*

"Thanks for your help and for writing your excellent book!" – *Laura Johnson*

"I have enjoyed reading your book and I've found excellent leads for finding ancestors." – *Donna Mann*

"… It is not only informative but entertaining. Incorporating your own experiences in brought the book to life. Again, thank you for helping me to understand the many aspects of genealogy and for supplying a roadmap to finding more information about our ancestors." – *Dana L. Hager*

"Of all the books I have looked at yours is the best…and you write with your heart and soul. Thanks for writing such a great book." – *Karen Dredge*

"I got this book out of the library, but before I was half-way through it, I decided I had to have my own copy. Lots of helpful suggestions! I'd recommend it for all new and experienced family historians." – *Margaret Combs*

"I am embarking on the family history journey and have found your book to be very helpful … thanks for putting together a helpful, easy to follow guide." – *Suzanne Adams*

"I'm absolutely delighted that I discovered your book "Secrets of Tracing Your Ancestors." I've only been at this for a month (to keep sane during knee surgery recuperation) and now I'm hooked." – *Cecily Bishop*

## About the Author

For more than 20 years, W. Daniel Quillen has been a professional writer specializing in travel and technical subjects. He has taught beginning genealogy courses to university students and working adults, and is a frequent lecturer in beginning and intermediate genealogy classes in Colorado. He has compiled his years of genealogical training and research into a series of genealogy how-to books, all available through www.essentialgenealogy.com. He lives in Centennial, Colorado with his wife and children. If you would like to contact Dan about anything in this book, his e-mail address is: wdanielquillen@gmail.com.

# MASTERING CENSUS & MILITARY RECORDS

Volume III of *Quillen's Essentials of Genealogy*
3rd Edition

www.essentialgenealogy.com

## W. Daniel Quillen

Author of *Secrets of Tracing Your Ancestors,*
*The Troubleshooter's Guide to Do-It-Yourself Genealogy,*
and *Quillen's Essentials of Genealogy* series

Cold Spring Press

# COLD SPRING PRESS

Quillen's Essentials of Genealogy series

www.essentialgenealogy.com

*Third Edition*

## PHOTO CREDITS

Cover design by Matthew Simmons (www.myselfincluded.com). Both cover images from flickr.com. Front cover image: scanmyoldphotos.com. Back cover image: freeparking. Page 8: Library of Congress.

# TABLE OF CONTENTS

# 1. INTRODUCTION

Welcome to your introduction to using census and military records in your genealogical research! If you are like most genealogists, even if you are just beginning your genealogical journey, you have probably already used census records to aid and abet your addiction to genealogy. So many of the United States genealogy records are now online via free and subscription services and are easily accessible; gone are the days of trips to Salt Lake City or to any of the fourteen National Archives locations, where you pore through rolls and rolls of microfilm, searching for your ancestors as though they were needles in ancestral haystacks.

Unlike census records, military records may represent a new area of research for you. Whether you are just beginning to use military records for research or are an experienced researcher and have used military records before, I hope to share some new tricks and information to aid you in your use of these most valuable records that are often chock full of genealogical data.

Sometimes, searching for your ancestors in censuses and military records will be easy – a veritable piece of cake. Other times it will take every ounce of detective skills you possess to ferret them out. Regardless of easy or hard, obvious or subtle, the journey will be exciting and the find exulting. There are so many nooks and crannies, unexpected turns and treasures in censuses and military records that I think you'll find the journey well worth your effort.

In addition to this book, which does a focused dive into the world of census and military records, there are several other books I recommend that might help round out your understanding of the world of genealogy:

**If you are a beginning genealogist**, you might consider picking up a book I wrote specifically for beginning genealogists – *Secrets of Tracing Your Ancestors*. *Secrets* will start you at the very beginning, with organization and where to find information close at hand, and takes you further along the various sources of genealogy. Reviewers have even observed that there are tactics and information in there that are good for experienced genealogists.

Learn from Dan's mistakes; don't repeat them!

**If you are a more experienced genealogist**, then you should consider picking up another of the genealogy books I have written: *Troubleshooter's Guide to Do-It-Yourself Genealogy*. It is targeted at those who have moved beyond the beginner's resources and are beginning to hit some real stumbling blocks in their research. It serves to provide you some sources you may not have been aware of, how to access them and how to get the most out of them.

Since this is the third in a series of books in the *Quillen's Essentials of Genealogy* series, you may also benefit from the other books in the series:

- *Mastering Online Genealogy*
- *Mastering Immigration & Naturalization Records*
- *Mastering Family, Library and Church Records*
- *Tracing Your European Roots*
- *Tracing Your Irish & British Records*

Okay – now that we're past the shameless self-marketing, let's get on with this book.

**Meet the Family**
As I have done in my previous books, I am going to introduce you to my family. Many of them have interesting stories unraveled only through research using

census and military records, and I will use them to teach you various and sundry techniques and sources that you will be able to use to find your own difficult-to-track-down ancestors! Along the way, I'll point out pitfalls and pratfalls that I have so easily wandered into along my genealogical journey, hopefully sparing you a bit of the same.

I am William Daniel Quillen, and I am married to the lovely Bonita Blau. We have six children.

My parents are:
William Edgar Quillen and Versie Lee Lowrance

My grandparents were:
•Helon Edgar Quillen and Vivian Iris Cunningham
•Elzie Lee Lowrance and Alma Hudson

My great grandparents were:
•Edgar Estil Quillen and Theodora Charity McCollough
•William Edward Cunningham and Emma Adelia Sellers
•Thomas Newton Lowrance and Margaret Ann McClure
•Francis Marion Hudson and Margaret Ellen Turpin

My 2nd great grandparents were:
•Jonathan Baldwin Quillen and Sarah Minerva Burke
•William Lindsay McCollough and Lucy Arabella Phillips
•William Huston Cunningham and Amanda Stunkard
•John Thomas Sellers and Celeste Elizabeth Horney
•Alpheus Marion Lowrance and Catherine Jemima Reece
•Jeremiah Hudson and Frances Duvall

My 3rd great grandparents were:
•Charles Franklin Quillen and Susan or Susannah _____
•Samuel McCollough and Elizabeth Throckmorton
•Oliver Sayers Phillips and Charity Graham

- Joseph Cunningham and Sarah Rogers
- Matthew Stunkard and Margaret Peoples
- John T. Sellers and Elizabeth Ritchey
- Leonidas Horney and Jane Crawford
- Francis Marion Hudson and Mary Magdalene Yates
- John E. Duvall, Jr. and Elizabeth _____

As you may readily conclude from the above information, even as involved in genealogical research as I am, I have been unable to fill in the complete information for all my ancestors in just these few generations. I have traced some family lines back to medieval Ireland, and still others barely make it back to the 18th century. Doubtless you have the same kinds of ancestors: those who make it easy to find them, others who like to make it a tantalizing game of cat-and-mouse, and still others who seemingly want nothing to do with your research efforts. Hopefully by the time you finish this book, you will have discovered techniques that will help you find even the most elusive of your ancestors!

So – if you're ready, let's jump right in!

Dan Quillen

August 2014

*"I seek dead people"* (with apologies to *The Sixth Sense*!)

# 2. THE ESSENTIALS

Perhaps this is the first step in your genealogical journey, or perhaps 10,000+ steps preceded it. If the latter is true, you'll know what follows in this chapter are the critical, essential elements to being a successful genealogist. If you are the former person – just taking your first steps in genealogy – learn the lessons in this chapter well or suffer the consequences! Many of them are in this book for the simple reason that I did not learn these lessons when I first started my genealogical journey, and I have had to retrace many of my steps to do penance for my headlong dash down the genealogical pike. I hope to save you some steps by pointing out a few essential elements of successful genealogical research to you.

If you have read any of the other books in the *Quillen's Essentials of Genealogy* series, much of this will sound familiar. You are welcome to skim through it to refresh your memory, or skip it totally – you have my permission to do so. If however, you have not perused any of those other books, I strongly suggest you spend a few minutes and familiarize yourself with the items in this chapter. To do so may just save you tons of time and aggravation. Not to do so…well, you get the point.

## The Basics

To be a viable structure, every building needs to be built with a strong foundation, quality materials and using sound building principles. Your genealogy research needs the same features – a strong foundation, solid materials, sound building principles, etc. If you do not have those features, you are asking for trouble down your family line.

Following are a few of the basic building blocks and tools with which you'll want to work while working on your genealogical house – the House of Quillan, Hudson House, Reilly Residence, Adams Abode, etc. This chapter is a bit of a free flowing

> Write down ALL sources, even hearsay and conjecture.

stream of consciousness of information. Not much rhyme or reason, but each snippet is an important one for you to remember and practice, lest you regret not having done so. The information in this chapter applies to your genealogical research, whether you are using censuses, military records, immigration and naturalization records, etc. I have just shared basics of the basics. As I mentioned earlier, if you want or need more on these topics, you can check out *Secrets of Tracing Your Ancestors*.

## Notes

First – keep notes. Good notes. Write down the source of every scrap and tidbit of genealogical information about your ancestors that comes your way. Even if it's a family story told you by your great aunt Ruth, write it down and record the source. Record the titles of books. If you found the book in a library, include the call numbers and where the book was located. Include the page numbers.

If you've found information on the internet, include not only the information but the URL of the website. Nothing is more frustrating than to have some great information in your notes about an ancestor, and you know it was from a website, and simply cannot recall what the name of the website is, much less the URL.

A few years ago I was poking around the Internet looking for my second great grandfather, Jonathan Baldwin Quillen. We knew he was born someplace near the confluence of the states of Virginia, Kentucky, Tennessee and North Carolina. An older relative thought she heard he had been born in Hawkins County, Tennessee, so I figured that was a good place to search.

After a bit of searching, I found a genealogy society for Hawkins County, Tennessee. On the genealogy society's home page, it listed the names of the society's members, and the surnames they were researching. Lo and behold, one of the members was doing research on Quillan / Quillen / Quillin family lines. I clicked on his name and was given his e-mail address. I immediately fired off an e-mail to him, and then turned my attention to scouring the Internet again.

The next day, I thought I would see if I could find the website again. Nothing. No matter how creative I got, I was unable to find the website for that genealogy society again. To this day, I don't know where it went. Had I written down the URL (or simply cut-and-pasted it into my genealogy software), I could have found it in a heartbeat!

URL = abbreviation for universal resource locator (aka uniform resource locator). Copy these down!

This was a good example of the reality that websites come up and go down all the time. They change names, service providers are changed resulting in a change of URL, etc.

Another good idea is to copy down the name of the owner / maintainer of the website – their names are usually listed along with their contact information and most often appear at the bottom of a web page. Occasionally their names appear in the *Contact Information* or *Contact Us* section. Had I done that with the Hawkins County, I could have contacted him / her to learn how to further access the site.

But don't worry about me – lucky for me (this time!), I had copied the e-mail address of the fellow who was researching the Quillen line. After I contacted him, he offered to share the research he had been doing on the Quillens for the past three decades. I was happy to accept it! The information he provided turned out to be a gold mine for me – over 3,600 ancestors with the surname Quillen, not to mention those families they married into.

**Be specific**
When you are contacting organizations and fellow genealogists, be specific in your requests. Don't make the mistake of saying:

"I am doing research on the Quillen family of Lee County, Virginia, and would like everything you have on that line."

That sort of a request will most likely yield a whole bunch of nothing, especially if you are contacting a government entity, like a county courthouse. A better – and more successful – approach is to be specific in your request:

"I am doing research on my great grandfather, Edgar Estil Quillen. I believe he was born in Lee County, Virginia on or about January 15, 1880 or 1881. His father was Jonathan Baldwin Quillen and his mother was Sarah Minerva Burke Quillen. I am seeking Edgar's birth certificate."

Or:

"I am trying to locate the will of my second great grandfather, Jonathan Baldwin Quillen. He died in Hartville, Wright County, Missouri on January 21, 1920."

**Speed vs. Accuracy**

When I do genealogy, like when I write, I always seem to feel a tremendous sense of urgency. Also, I get manic whenever I write or do genealogy – I can work at a thrilling pace for hours on end, and when I am finished, it seems that no more than 30 or 40 minutes have passed. When I am doing genealogy research, it seems as though I just can't get to information quickly enough, and when I find it, I seem compelled to record it as rapidly as possible. In so doing, I am chagrined to say, I have made far too many errors in recording dates, places, spellings of names, etc. Slow down, take your time, and record the information accurately – the spelling of his name, her birth date and place, etc. And then check and recheck to make sure you recorded all the information accurately.

Measure twice, cut once.

As you are building your genealogical house, use the advice my father gave me years ago for construction projects: *measure twice, cut once*. As it applies to genealogical research, careful attention to detail is crucial.

**Standard Dating Format**

My wife always gives me a hard time when we go out to eat. I prefer going to the same restaurants, and having the same entrée; she prefers different restaurants, or if we do go to some of our favorite restaurants, she tries something different each time. It drives her slightly wacky that I don't share her sense of dining adventure. And so it is with dating formats for your genealogical research. There are several formats you could use, but I recommend one and one only. This may sound a bit obsessive (I have been accused of that on occasion), but you should use this one format absolutely consistently without deviation. Get used to recording your dates as: day / month / year in the following format – DD/MON/YYYY. For example: 1 January 2011, or 1 Jan 2011. Avoid the shortcut of listing dates as 1/11/11. If you write a date in such a fashion, did you mean:

January 11, 2011? January 11, 1911? January 11, 1811??

Or

November 1, 2011? November 1, 1911? November 1, 1811?

I guarantee that no matter how much you think you will remember what date you meant to write down, when you revisit that date months or years from now, you'll say to yourself: "What was I thinking?!"

The standard dating convention among genealogists is DD/MM (either spelled out or the first three letters)/YYYY. It works well and clears up a lot of potential confusion and mistakes.

**Don't give up**
There's an old maxim floating out there: "The hurrier I go, the further behind I get."

Sometimes you will hit a brick wall. Every courthouse, every marriage record, birth registry, etc., just comes up empty for an ancestor you know was living in that town or county. Step back, take a deep breath, and maybe even turn your attention to someone else. New records are coming online daily. What wasn't there today may be there tomorrow. Or next month. Or next year.

In the genealogy research I have done, I have seen a pattern develop for those who seem particularly difficult to find. I have noticed that if I step back and turn my attention to other individuals, the person I have been seeking unsuccessfully realizes they have lost my attention, and it bothers them. They decide that rather than be left completely behind, they'll throw me a morsel of information – as I search for other family members, I'll find a partial birth date for the abandoned individual, or a mention of them in a sister's will or obituary. You may scoff at the suggestion that this happens, but I have personally experienced it time and time again, and many genealogists with whom I have spoken will vouch for its reality.

As I was writing this book, I was discussing the progress a fellow researcher was making – or not – on a Danish immigrant ancestor of his. Try as he might, he was unsuccessful at every turn at locating accurate information on this individual. So he turned his attention elsewhere. Within a very short time, this friend's daughter was doing her own genealogy research. She returned a book to the shelves at the library, and as she was walking down an aisle lined with books filled with information on Danish immigrants, her attention was drawn to a specific book among many on a particular shelf. Acting on the hunch (prompting? feeling? intuition?) she grabbed the book and opened it at random. Lo and behold, there was the information on this immigrant ancestor that had been eluding her and her father for years. The information proved to be accurate, it cleared up some mysteries that had cropped up about the individual and his family, and even extended that line back several more generations.

Perhaps another example will suffice. I had been searching for the birth information for a great aunt of mine. Family tradition (and my Aunt Ruth!) said that she was born in Cottonwood Falls, Kansas. A search of vital records there turned up her three brothers, but not her. One time when I was fresh off another disappointing dead end on this great aunt, I was visiting my folks while on a business trip to Colorado. While I was there, my grandfather's three sisters and a cousin dropped in for a visit. I once again asked my Aunt Ruth about Aunt Agnes, and she confirmed her understanding that Agnes was born in Cottonwood Falls, Kansas. At that point, the cousin (whom I had never before met, nor have I seen since) piped up and said that No, Agnes hadn't been born in Cottonwood Falls, and that the family moved there when she was a little girl. She thought they had lived in Sharon

Springs, Kansas before moving to Cottonwood Falls. A search of the county birth records for Sharon Springs confirmed it as the birthplace of my Aunt Agnes.

When my great aunts and their cousin – three octogenarians and one septuagenarian! – dropped by for a visit with my folks, I just happened to have been there from my home in New Jersey. My great aunts had driven up unannounced from Oklahoma to visit my parents' Denver home, and had invited this information-bearing cousin to accompany them at the last minute.

The key is not to give up completely. It's okay to set a research project aside for a time, but be sure and return to it and check if any new sources have become available. Also, be sensitive to information that might pop up at the most unexpected moments and in the most unexpected ways.

**The Journey**
There are many ways of getting to where you're going, and you have to learn what works best for you. If you don't mind, I'll liken your genealogical research to a journey, a journey to locate your ancestors.

> Be open to unexpected sources of information.

What kind of a traveler are you? Are you the type that believes the shortest distance between two locations is a straight line? Do you jump on the highway, and get there as fast as you can? Or are you more of a meanderer?

Perhaps your research will take on your personal traveling characteristics. You may become so focused on a particular ancestor that you pass others by, others who might fill out your family tree and lead you to the elusive ancestor on whom you were focused. Brothers, sisters, aunts, uncles, cousins, grandparents, etc., may yield results about your target ancestor through their wills (*I leave to my nephew Jonathan Baldwin Quillen...*) or obituaries (Priscilla Quillen Collingsworth is survived by two brothers, Jonathan of Hartville MO and Jimmy of Estilville, VA). The same goes for the social pages of old newspapers (*Mrs. Priscilla Collingsworth's brother Jonathan Quillen and his wife Sarah visited this week from their home in Hartville, Missouri.*)

> Don't be in such a hurry that you miss important information.

Don't be so focused on another ancestor that you miss some information; slow down and enjoy the familial scenery that passes by as you pursue that elusive ancestor, and you may find clues that will help you end the chase for the Elusive One.

But – don't get lost in the trees! Sometimes you can get so distracted following the thread of a trail for another ancestor that you completely lose track of the main purpose of your search – to find your second great grandfather's birth certificate. More than once I have found myself following leads like the thread that took me to my great grandfather's son's wife's family. Yes, they are family – of a sort. Yes, I will probably want to capture their information some day. But if I spend hours and hours chasing and recording information about them, those are hours that I have been diverted from my true goal – a birth certificate of one of my progenitors.

## Research Plan

To avoid getting lost in the woods (see above), especially if you find yourself to be one of those genealogists who takes a lot of detours (I am guilty of this!) during your research, it might be really wise for you to develop a research plan. It can be as formal or as informal as you like. Handwritten or typed, detailed or high-level, whatever you find works best for you. At a minimum, here are some of the things that should go in your research plan:

• The name of the person for whom you are searching
• The information you are seeking for that person – birth or death date, marriage date and / or spouse, death date, etc.
• Likely location
• Resources thought to be available

> Plan your work – work your plan!

Understand, a Research Plan can be much, much more than this. It just depends on how detailed you want or need to get to keep you focused.

When I research, my personal preference is not to have the journey laid out so perfectly that I miss some wonderful scenery along the way. Here's an easy, not-too-detailed research plan that has worked time and again for me. The details change (names, locations, ancillary lines, etc.), but the format's usually very consistent:

| | |
|---|---|
| **Research Goal** | Find the birth date for Jonathan Baldwin Quillen |
| **Probable location(s)** | Sullivan Co, TN, Hawkins Co., TN, Hancock Co, TN, Lee Co., VA |
| **Associated surnames** | Burke (wife's maiden name), |
| **Possible resources** | Vital records for above counties, TN State Library & Archives, VA State Library & Archives, county genealogy society websites, |
| **Comments** | I have three dates for JB's birth date: 18 May 1845, 21 May 1845, and 17 September 1845. |

**Privacy Laws**

I'll address privacy from several positions. First, there are laws governing the privacy of an individual's information. These should of course be adhered to. The government makes this easy on you as far as censuses go – they are not released until 72 years after the census enumeration date.

In addition to legal restrictions on sharing information such as birth, marriage and death records, there are also common courtesies that should apply regarding privacy. Let me provide you with an example.

When I was beginning my genealogical journey, I became an early convert to the value and genealogic power of censuses. The plethora of information found there is exciting. I realized the information was almost all a secondary source, but it helped me visualize the families on whom I was doing research – and often enabled me to find primary sources. In particular, I had been thrilled to find my great grandfather and his family in several consecutive censuses. Francis Marion Hudson was known within the family as "Papa," and was reported to have ruled the roost with a bit of an iron fist — not abusive, just pretty much the situation of there being no question about who was the head honcho in the family. So strong was his influence that my grandmother had to sneak off to get married because Papa didn't approve of her sweetheart – my grandfather. After their marriage, they lived in Texas for several years, away from the family, for fear of the consequences of returning to an unhappy Papa. Here are a couple of the census entries for my great grandfather:

Here Francis M. is as a rambunctious two-year-old in the Moreland Township, Pope County Arkansas 1880 census:

The 1890 census was lost in a fire, but here's my great grandfather in the 1900 census for Comanche, Oklahoma Indian Territory. He had apparently moved from his parents' home and was a 22-year-old laborer for James Martin:

And here he is with his wife and a couple of brothers-in-law in the 1910 census for King Township, located in Stephens County, Oklahoma. Note according to the census, he and his wife had been married less than a year (see the 0 listed in the column that says *Number of years of present marriage*):

Whoa! This census indicated that my great grandfather had been married once before he married my great grandmother! (Note the $M^2$ in the *Whether single, married, widowed or divorced* column, indicating this was his second marriage!) This was news to me, and as far as I knew, to the rest of the family. I was concerned about how to handle this information, as I wasn't certain my grandmother, in particular, knew about this previous marriage of her father. I wasn't even sure my own mother was aware of this information.

My mother's sister, my aunt Carol, shares some of my interest in genealogy. It was she to whom I turned to check the information out. She confirmed the information, and even seemed to recall the name of my great grandfather's first wife. She recalled it had been marriage of young loves that didn't last even a year.

All that to say – be careful with the information you find that might be of a sensitive nature. More than one instance in my family history tells of out-of-wedlock births (or at least births within several months of marriage), divorces, illegal activity, etc.

# 3. U.S. CENSUS HISTORY

Census. Zensus. Censo. Censimento. Recensement. Sítání. Folkräkning.

No matter what your immigrant ancestors may have called them, censuses represent a major undertaking of the government, and genealogists benefit greatly from their efforts. Crammed full of genealogically relevant information, these instruments originally grew from an effort to accurately tax the inhabitants of the United States and to establish the number of Representatives each state would have in the House of Representatives. Over time, the government expanded the information they were seeking, and the census as an informational instrument provided a decade-by-decade snapshot of the demographics of our country – not to mention a valuable resource for genealogists.

---

**United States Census Established**

One of the seminal documents of our nation's history is the US Constitution, and one of the first things provided for was a census. A scant 176 words into the Constitution, we find Article I, Section 2, Clause 3, which reads:

*Representatives and direct Taxes shall be apportioned among the several States which may be included within this Union, according to their respective Numbers, which shall be determined by adding to the whole Number of free Persons, including those bound to Service for a Term of Years, and excluding Indians not taxed, three fifths of all other Persons....The actual Enumeration shall be made within three Years after the first Meeting of the Congress of the United States, and within every subsequent Term of ten Years, in such Manner as they shall by Law direct. The Number of Representatives shall not exceed one for every thirty Thousand, but each State shall have at Least one Representative....*

---

Beginning in 1790 and extending to present day, censuses prove a valuable tool for genealogists. States got into the act too, and often conducted their own censuses – population, agriculture, industrial, etc. (more on those censuses later).

Thomas Jefferson was the third president of our nation. His reputation is one of incredible intelligence – drafter of the Declaration of Independence and founder of the University of Virginia. One of the reasons for his intelligence came from an intense intellectual curiosity. That intellectual curiosity caused him to send Lewis and Clark on their grand adventure of the newly acquired lands of the Louisiana Purchase. His curiosity also caused the census instrument to evolve from the taxation instrument it was originally intended to be to a means of finding out more about the American populace. He indicated he wanted to use the census to learn "…a more detailed view of the inhabitants of the country." His leadership in this area set a precedent for the census to be used for more than simple enumeration, and over time, it has evolved to provide more than numbers: names, ages, relationships, vocation, disability, literacy, ethnicity, birth information, etc.

**Questions, Questions, Questions**
Since its initial inception as a tally system, the census evolved, and additional questions that were of interest to the government were added. Following are the various questions that were asked for each census:

**1790 — Enumeration date 2 August 1790**
• Head of family
• Free white males
• 16 and up, including head of family
• Under 16
• Free white females
• Including head
• All other persons
• Slaves
• County
• City

Note: No schedules are known to exist for the 1790 Census for Delaware, Georgia, Kentucky, New Jersey, Tennessee, and Virginia. It is thought they were destroyed during the War of 1812 when the British attacked Washington. Some Virginia records are available from state enumeration records taken in 1790.

**1800 — Enumeration date 4 August 1800**
• Head of family
• Free white males
• Under 10
• 10 to 16
• 16 to 26
• 26 to 45
• 45 and over
• Free white females
• Under 10
• 10 to 16
• 16 to 26
• 26 to 45
• 45 and over
• All others
• Slaves
• Remarks

**1810 — Enumeration date 6 August 1810**
(Same as 1800)

**1820 — Enumeration date 7 August 1820**
• Head of family
• Free white males
• Under 10
• 10 to 16
• 16 to 18
• 16 to 26
• 26 to 45

- 45 and over
- Free white females
- Under 10
- 10 to 16
- 16 to 18
- 16 to 26
- 26 to 45
- 45 and over
- Foreigners not naturalized
- Agriculture
- Commerce
- Manufacturers
- Free coloreds
- Slaves
- Remarks

**1830 — Enumeration date 1 June 1830**
- Head of family
- Free white males
- Under 5, 5 to 10, 10 to 15, 15 to 20, 20 to 30, 30 to 40, 40 to 50, 50 to 60, 60 to 70, 70 to 80, 80 to 90, 90 to 100, over 100
- Free white females
- Under 5, 5 to 10, 10 to 15, 15 to 20, 20 to 30, 30 to 40, 40 to 50, 50 to 60, 60 to 70, 70 to 80, 80 to 90, 90 to 100, over 100
- Slaves
- Free colored

**1840 – Enumeration Date 1 June 1840**
(Same as 1830)

**1850 – Enumeration Date 1 June 1850**
- Name
- Age
- Sex

- Color
- Occupation
- Value of real estate
- Birthplace
- Married within year
- School within year
- Cannot read or write
- Enumeration date
- Remarks

## 1860 – Enumeration Date 1 June 1860

- Name
- Age
- Sex
- Color
- Occupation
- Value of real estate
- Value of personal property
- Birthplace
- Married in year
- School in year
- Cannot read or write
- Enumeration date
- Remarks

## 1870 – Enumeration date 1 June 1870

- Name
- Age
- Sex
- Color
- Occupation
- Value of real estate
- Value of personal property
- Birthplace

- Father foreign born
- Mother foreign born
- Month born in census year
- School in census year
- Can't read or write
- Eligible to vote
- Date of enumeration

**1880 — Enumeration date 1 June 1880**

- Name
- Color
- Sex
- Age June 1 in census year
- Relationship to head of house
- Single
- Married
- Widowed
- Divorced
- Married in census year
- Occupation
- Other information
- Can't read or write
- Place of birth
- Place of birth of father
- Place of birth of mother
- Enumeration date

**1890 — Enumeration date 1 June 1890**

Note: Tragically, the vast majority of the 1890 Census was destroyed in a fire (or by the water that was used to put out the fire!). A few census records survived, and a number of parties have cobbled together information about the 1890 population through various Indian Territory schedules, city directories, 1890 veteran schedules, etc.

**1900 — Enumeration date 1 June 1900**
• Name of each person whose place of abode on June 1, 1900 was in this family
• Relation to head of family
• Sex
• Color
• Month of birth
• Year of birth
• Age
• Marital status
• Number of years married
• Mother of how many children
• Number of these children living
• Place of birth
• Place of birth of father
• Place of birth of mother
• Years of immigration to US
• Number of years in US
• Naturalization
• Occupation
• Number of months not employed
• Attended school (months)
• Can read
• Can write
• Can speak English
• Home owned or rented
• Home owned free or mortgaged
• Farm or house

**Note** that the 1900 US census asks for the month and year of birth. This may be very helpful in identifying a primary source (like a birth certificate) for this person.

**1910 — Enumeration date 15 April 1910**
• Name of each person whose place of abode on April 15, 1910 was in this family
• Relation to head of family

- Sex
- Race
- Age
- Marital status
- Number of years married
- Mother of how many children
- Number of these children living
- Place of birth
- Place of birth of father
- Place of birth of mother
- Years of immigration to US
- Naturalized or alien
- Language spoken
- Occupation
- Nature of trade
- Employer, worker or own account
- Number of months not employed
- Can read and write
- Attending school
- Home owned or rented
- Home owned free or mortgaged
- Farm or house
- Whether a survivor of the Union or Confederate Army or Navy
- Blind or deaf-mute

**1920 — Enumeration date 1 January 1920**
- Name of each person whose place of abode on January 1, 1920 was in this family
- Relation to head of family
- Home owned or rented
- Home owned free or mortgaged
- Sex
- Color or race
- Age
- Marital status

- Years of immigration to US
- Naturalized or alien
- Year of naturalization
- Attending school
- Can read or write
- Place of birth
- Mother tongue
- Place of birth of father
- Mother tongue of father
- Place of birth of mother
- Mother tongue of mother
- Can speak English
- Occupation

**1930 — Enumeration date 1 April 1930**
- Name of each person whose place of abode on April 1, 1930 was in this family
- Relationship of this person to the head of the family
- Home owned or rented
- Value of home, if owned, or monthly rental, if rented
- Radio set
- Does this family own a farm?
- Color or race
- Age at last birthday
- Marital condition
- Age at first marriage
- Attended school or college any time since Sept. 1, 1929
- Whether able to read or write
- Place of birth
- Place of birth of father
- Place of birth of mother
- Mother tongue (or native language) of foreign born
- Year of immigration into the United States
- Naturalization
- Whether able to speak English

- Trade, profession, or particular kind of work done
- Industry or business
- Class of worker
- Whether actually at work yesterday
- Whether a veteran of U.S. Military or naval forces
- What war or expedition
- Number of farm schedule

**1940 — Enumeration date 1 April 1940**
- Address (number and street)
- Name of each person whose place of abode on April 1, 1940 was in this family
- Relationship of this person to the head of the family
- Home owned or rented
- Value of home, if owned, or monthly rental, if rented
- Radio set
- Does this household live on a farm?
- Color or race
- Age at last birthday
- Marital condition
- Age at first marriage
- Attended school or college any time since March 1, 1940
- Highest grade of school completed
- Whether able to read or write
- Place of birth
- Citizenship of the foreign born
- Whether a veteran of U.S. military or naval forces
- Whether wife, widow or under-18-year-old child of a veteran
- Veterans – war or military service
- Residence on April 1, 1935
- Employment status (ten questions on employment status)
- Income in 1939
- Place of birth of father
- Place of birth of mother
- Mother tongue (or native language) of foreign born

- Usual occupation
- Usual industry
- Income earned in 1939
- For all women who are or have been married:
  - Has this woman been married more than once
  - Age at first marriage
  - Number of children ever born (do not include stillbirths)
- Number of farm schedule

As you work with censuses, bear in mind that enumeration dates varied census to census. Keeping this in mind will help explain why an ancestor only aged nine (or maybe even eleven!) years between censuses. For example, let's say you have an ancestor who was born January 18, 1880. The 1920 census says he is 39. But in the 1930 census he is 50. Hmmm – how could that be? The 1920 census was enumerated as of January 1, 1920, and the 1930 census was enumerated as of April 1, 1930. In 1920, your ancestor would have turned 40 two weeks after the enumeration date, while he would have turned 50 a little over two months before the date of enumeration for the 1930 census. Sometimes different enumeration dates will be the explanation for age discrepancies. Other times there were other reasons: dimming memories, neighbor's guesses, younger children's guesses, etc. I have listed the enumeration dates for each of the censuses above; but here's a handy guide for you:

> Pay attention to enumeration dates! They were not uniform from census to census.

**First Monday in August:**
1790 (2 August)
1800 (4 August)
1810 (6 August)
1820 (7 August)

**1 June:**
1830 through 1900

**15 April:**
1910

**1 January:**
1920

**1 April:**
1930
1940

## The Enumerators

Censuses depended on enumerators – people hired to go from house to house to glean all the information that particular decade's census was asking. Genealogists owe a lot to these road warriors – their efforts have added uncounted and invaluable volumes of data to the information available on our ancestors. Owing to a scarcity of vital records as we go back in US history, the information these stalwarts gleaned on our ancestors may very well be the only information we ever find on them.

In addition to a genealogist, I am also a history buff. I love history, and love learning about the past. At the confluence of those two loves (genealogy and history), I sought information on enumerators: Who were they? How did they do it? How much were they paid? What instructions did they receive? Following are some of the answers I have gleaned through the years:

**Who were they?** Initially, they were the tax collectors. Recall that the early censuses were revenue tools with little genealogical value. The tax assessor or local marshal was often tasked with enumerating their districts for the census. As the population grew and more questions were asked, individuals were hired specifically as enumerators. The earliest censuses (1790 to 1870) provided for enumerators to gather information over a period of from five to eighteen months. Beginning with the 1880 census, enumerators were given one month to cover their districts.

**How did they do it?** They were to go house to house, farm to farm.

**How much were they paid?** I found an article in a newspaper from 1900 that shed a little light on that:

> *A minimum rate of two cents for each living inhabitant, two cents for each death, fifteen cents for each farm, twenty cents for each establishment of productive industry is provided for all subdivisions where such allowance shall be deemed sufficient....The compensation allowed to enumerators will be not less than three nor more than six dollars per day of ten hours actual field work. (Work on The Census - How Appointments are Made in The News, Frederick, Maryland, February 7, 1900.)*

In 1790, enumerators received $1.00 for every 150 persons enumerated. If their district was a city with more than 5,000 people, they received $1.00 for every *300* persons enumerated.

Compensation for enumerators was set by Congress for each census. The 2010 census allowed regional census administrators to set the rates, but they generally ranged between $8.25 and $18.50 per hour, depending on the location.

**What instructions did enumerators receive?** In 1890, enumerators were given the following instructions:

> *DUTIES OF ENUMERATORS:*
> *It is the duty of each enumerator...to visit personally each dwelling in his subdivision, and each family therein, and each individual living out of a family in any place of abode, and by inquiry made of the head of such family, or of the member thereof deemed most credible and worthy of trust, and of such individual living out of a family, to obtain each and every item of information and all the particulars required by the act of March 1, 1889. All of this data is to be obtained as of date June 1, 1890.*

> *In case no person shall be found at the usual place of abode of such family, or individual living out of a family, competent to answer the inquiries made in compliance with the requirements of the act, then it shall be lawful for the enumerator to obtain the required information, as nearly as may be practicable, from the family or families, or person or persons, living nearest to such place of abode....*

> *It is the prime object of the enumeration to obtain the name and the requisite particulars as to personal description of every person in the United States, except Indians not taxed.*

To put the pay the enumerators received in perspective, here are the costs of a few items from 1900:

Butter — $.25 / pound
Lemons — $.15 / dozen
Maple Syrup — $.90 / gallon
Sausage — $.12 / pound
Rib roast — $.10 / pound
Floor wax — $.75 / gallon
Flower pot — $.02 each
Lawn Mower — $2.35
Newspaper — $.01 for a daily newspaper

In addition, enumerators were warned that shirking their duties or falsifying information could result in fines and / or imprisonment. They were told to be polite, but not to allow people to be rude to them. The enumerator was to be "...*prompt, rapid*, and *decisive* in announcing his object and his authority and in making his inquiries, but in so doing he should not arouse any antagonism or give any offense..."

Enumerators were cautioned that sometimes families wouldn't be truthful about disabilities (deaf, blind, etc.) of family members, particularly children. If the enumerator knew personally of such a condition, or was told by someone credible (a neighbor, for instance), they were to record the correct data.

And finally, they were warned that they must keep all information gathered private and not share it with unauthorized individuals. To do so could net the enumerator a fine of up to $500, a considerable sum in 1890.

So a special thanks are owed to all census enumerators!

Similar instructions were provided to enumerators for each census. If you're interested (they really are fascinating reading), you can find copies of the instructions for enumerators of each census at *www.census.gov/history/www/through_the_decades/census_instructions/*.

# 4. GETTING THE MOST OUT OF CENSUSES

Now that you've learned a little of the history of censuses, let's move forward and learn how to use them effectively.

**Beware the errors**

Before you travel this genealogical research path, here's a critical point: as wonderful a source as censuses are, they are frequently incorrect. Names are spelled incorrectly, ages are wrong, birth places change from census to census, etc., etc.

For years I have tried to understand why censuses are fraught with error. Why were so many of the names in the censuses misspelled? Or why an individual only ages 8 years, or perhaps 12 years, from census to census? I have concluded it was most likely a combination of things. Perhaps the family wasn't home and the enumerator asked a neighbor about the family. Perhaps a vicious dog prevented the enumerator from approaching the house, so the enumerator asked a neighbor. Literacy being what it was (or wasn't!), perhaps enumerators were left to guess at the spelling of individuals' names – first as well as surname – since the family had no idea how to spell them. Maybe no adults were around, and the enumerator asked the young son or daughter about family information. I suspect all of the above, and many more reasons I haven't even thought of, are the reasons for the errors in spelling, dates, ages, etc. Family legend has it that one of my great grandmothers always claimed she was born in Arkansas because she was embarrassed to admit that she was born in Texas! (Sorry to my readers from the Lone Star state!) Regardless of the reason, this is an important element of working with censuses you would do well to remember.

Let me share a fairly common example. To illustrate, I'll use my great grandparents, Thomas Newton and Margaret Ann McClure Lowrance. The information I have on Thomas is that he was born 19 January 1873 in Arkansas and that his father was born in Tennessee and his mother in North Carolina. Margaret (Maggie) was born 4 May 1876 and her parents were both born in Missouri. Here is the information provided for Thomas and Maggie through the census years:

**1880,** *enumeration date 1 June 1880*
Lowrance, Thomas N. age 6, born Arkansas, father born Tennessee, mother born North Carolina.

McClure, Maggie, age 4, born Texas, father born Missouri, mother born Missouri

We discover our first discrepancy: the enumeration date for the 1880 census was 1 June, 1880, and both Thomas and Maggie should have had their birthdays (Thomas in January, Maggie in May). But if Thomas was born in January 1873, he should have been 7 as of the 1 June, 1880 enumeration date.

**1890** *(lost in a fire)*

**1900,** *enumeration date 1 June, 1900*
Lowrance, Thomas N., age 27, born Arkansas, father born Tennessee, mother born North Carolina.

McClure, Margaret A., age 24, born Arkansas, father born Missouri, mother born Missouri.

Here we discover Margaret's birthplace moving from Texas to Arkansas...hmmm, maybe there is something to that family legend.

**1910,** *enumeration date 15 April, 1910*
Lowrance, T N, age 37, born Arkansas, father born Kentucky, mother born Kentucky.

McClure, Maggie A., age 33, born Arkansas, father born Missouri, mother born Missouri.

Another discrepancy – the 1910 census shows both Thomas's parents born in Kentucky, rather than in Tennessee and North Carolina, as in earlier censuses.

Maggie's age – 33 – as of the enumeration date lends credence to the May 1876 birth date I have for her. Had her birth date been prior to 15 April 1910 – the enumeration date – then her age would have been 34.

**1920**, *enumeration date 1 January 1920*
Lourance, Tomas N., age 46, born Arkansas, father born North Carolina, mother born North Carolina.

McClure, Maggie, age 43, born Arkansas, father born US, mother born US.

Note the misspellings of Thomas's first and last names. Also, this census says his father was born in North Carolina, not Tennessee. The birth places for Maggie's parents are simply listed as US. Based on the birth dates I have for both Thomas and Maggie, their ages are correct for this census – Thomas would turn 47 in January 1920 and Maggie would turn 44 in May 1920.

**1930**, *enumeration date 1 April 1930*
Lowrance, Thomas N., age 57, born Arkansas, father born Tennessee, mother born North Carolina.

McClure, Maggie A., age 53, born Texas, father born Arkansas, mother born Arkansas.

Again, ages for Thomas and Maggie are correct, given their respective birth dates and the enumeration date of the 1930 census. Thomas's parents' birth places are again shown as Tennessee and North Carolina. However, Maggie's birth place is given as Texas and her parents are now shown as being both born in Arkansas!

In summary, here is the information we have across four censuses for this American couple:

• Thomas always shows as being born in Arkansas.
• Thomas's father is shown as being born in Tennessee, North Carolina and Kentucky.
• Thomas's mother is shown as being born in North Carolina and Missouri.
• Maggie shows as being born in Arkansas and Texas
• Maggie's father is shown as being born in Missouri, the US and Arkansas.
• Maggie's mother is shown as being born in Missouri, the US and Arkansas.
• Thomas's first and last names were both misspelled once.
• Generally speaking, their reported ages were correct based on other information I have, except for Thomas's age at the time of the 1880 census.

So, as you can see, while here is a great deal of genealogically significant data available through these four censuses, there are a number of discrepancies. Just be cautious as you use this information.

> Censuses often contain errors. Be cautious with the information found there.

So why use censuses, if we know going in that there is a high likelihood that some of the information is incorrect? Well, I can think of a few reasons; they tell you:

• where a family was at a specific time and place;
• who family members were at that time and place;
• at least approximate ages of your family members on the date of the enumeration;
• other family members who may have been living close by;
• a missing spouse or child from one census to the next may indicate a death;
• a missing older child may indicate a marriage had taken place between censuses.

And so on. Also, the information you find on censuses may help you narrow your search for your ancestors in more reliable sources, such as marriage registers, birth certificates, etc. They may provide a short range of years within which to look for information, or a city or state (or country) that should be searched for vital records, etc. And it is entirely possible that censuses may well be the only information you will ever find on this particular family, or on certain family members.

So let's get started.

**Where to look for censuses?** Ten or fifteen years ago, the answer to this question would have been different than it is today. Back then, if you were going to do census research, you would most likely have been relegated to searching page after microfilm page of censuses at a facility that provided microfilm readers – state and genealogy libraries, the LDS Church Family History Library in Salt Lake City, Utah, or National Archives locations.

Thankfully, things have changed. The Internet and digital technology have made most of the censuses available from the comfort of our homes. Ancestry.com, Fold3 and HeritageQuest.com have made searching the censuses much easier by putting them online as well as providing indexes for the censuses. Without indexes, even with digitized census pages available on the Internet, you would still have to view page after page in the Enumeration District where you believed your ancestors lived.

Beginning in 1850, the censuses asked for the names and ages of each individual in the household. Prior to that, only the head of the family was listed, along with a numeric tally of the other people living in the household as of the enumeration date. No names were provided for those other individuals, but they were placed into a series of categories by age and sex.

Researching those earlier censuses (1790 through 1840) requires a bit of analysis and deduction. As an example of what I mean, I'll use my third great grandparents and their family. In the second chapter of this book, I introduced you to my family members, including Joseph and Sarah Rogers Cunningham. Below is the information I have on their family:

• Joseph Cunningham, born about 1791

- Sarah Rogers Cunningham, born about 1791
- Elisa Cunningham, born about 1814
- John Cunningham, born about 1816
- James Cunningham, born about 1817
- David Cunningham, born about 1821
- Rachel Cunningham, born about 1823
- Joseph Cunningham, born about 1826
- William Huston Cunningham, born 12 April 1828
- Jehu Cunningham, born about 1830
- Samuel Cunningham, born about 1832
- Andrew Cunningham, born about 1834
- Sarah Cunningham, born about 1836

Now, here is the 1830 census for that same family:

*1830 Census — Tuscarora Township, Mifflin County, Pennsylvania*
Head of Family: Joseph Cunningham
2 males under 5 years, 0 females 5 to 10 years
2 males 5 to 10 years, 1 female 5 to 10 years
2 males 10 to 15 years, 0 females 10 to 15 years
0 males 15 to 20 years, 1 female 15 to 20 years
1 male 30 to 40 years, 1 female 30 to 40 years

So based on this census and a little deductive reasoning, on 1 April 1830, the Joseph Cunningham family consisted of:

- Joseph, who was between 30 and 40 years of age
- A wife (probably) who was between 30 and 40 years of age
- Six sons and two daughters in the age ranges indicated.

Using your detective and analytic skills, you might reasonably assume the following individuals in each category, based on the census and the other information I had:

- Head of Family: Joseph Cunningham

- 2 males under 5 years, 0 females 5 to 10 years – William Huston and Jehu
- 2 males 5 to 10 years, 1 female 5 to 10 years – Joseph and David, Rachel
- 2 males 10 to 15 years, 0 females 10 to 15 years – John and James
- 0 males 15 to 20 years, 1 female 15 to 20 years — Elisa
- 1 male 30 to 40 years, 1 female 30 to 40 years – Joseph and Sarah

Of course, the last three children – Samuel, Andrew and Sarah – were born after the 1830 census was taken, so they do not appear in the census.

Piece of cake, right? Well, actually, I was fortunate in that I had information on this family from the center section of a family Bible. My great grandmother (the granddaughter-in-law of Joseph Cunningham) had written to all the members of the family on hers and her husband's lines, and asked for genealogy information for each of those families. She then transferred that information into the family Bible. The information she gathered included names, ages, dates of birth, marriage and death, etc. What a boon for my research on those family lines! Using that information I was able to piece together this family and identify them with some certainty in the 1830 census.

By the time the 1850 census rolled around, I was unable to find a census listing Joseph and Sarah. In 1850, they would have been in their late 50s, so it is not unreasonable to assume they were still living. I was able to find most of their children in the 1850 census, but not all of them. Lacking a census record for them, I have to be open to the idea they may have died, however. Before I make that decision, however, I will continue my search for them.

> You must apply analytic and deductive reasoning to the 1790 through 1840 censuses since only the head of household was listed.

Hitting a stumbling block on Joseph and Sarah, I transferred my interest and research to their son and my second great grandfather: William Huston Cunningham. From the genealogy information I have in the family Bible, I know he married Miss Amanda Stunkard in November 1855, so the first time I am likely to find them as a couple is in the 1860 census. Here is what I have from our family Bible for the William Huston Cunningham family:

- William Huston Cunningham, b. 12 April 1828
- Amanda Stunkard Cunningham, b. 31 January 1834
- Sarah Lovina Belle Cunningham, b. 21 February 1857
- Rachel Joan Cunningham, b. 15 May 1859
- George Elmer Cunningham, b. 29 August, 1861
- Margaret Elisa Cunningham, b. 8 October 1863
- William Edward Cunningham, b. 25 December 1865
- John Furgeson Cunningham, b. 21 May 1869
- Effie Jenette Cunningham, b. 24 September 1873

Based on the above information, I will look for a Cunningham family with William or William H. as the head of the household and Amanda as the wife, with two daughters (Sarah and Rachel). Below is the 1860 census record for Wells Township, Fulton County, Pennsylvania:

- Cunningham, William H.,      age 30
    Amanda,          age 28
    Sarah L. B.,      age  3
    Rachel,          age  1

Score! Especially with the eldest daughter named Sarah L. B. – not much doubt she is Sarah Lovina Belle Cunningham! Ah, but there is a bit of a conundrum here. With a birthday of 12 April 1828, William H. should be 32, not 30. Remember – the 1860 census was enumerated as of 1 June 1860, so William would already have had his birthday in 1860. We'll have to watch future censuses and see if his age changes, or if we need to re-think the other (family Bible) information we have for him. Same for Amanda – had she been born in January 1834, then she should have been 26 in 1860...maybe she borrowed two years from William! (More likely, neighbors or other family members guessed their ages for the enumerator...) The ages for Sarah and Rachel agree with the information I have on them. Let's see how this plays out among other censuses.

Checking the 1870 census for Wells Township, Fulton County, Pennsylvania, we find...nothing. Okay – not to worry. They probably moved. Checking the 1870 census for all of Pennsylvania, we find…nothing. Hmmm. There are several possibilities and options to consider. First, they're probably too young to have all died. Second, I was checking the census index for William, but can't find him. So I search census indexes in Pennsylvania just for Amanda – perhaps William died between 1860 and 1870. I check for Amanda and that yields nothing. I search for a Sarah as well as Rachel in census indexes for Pennsylvania and find nothing. So I shift my focus, open to the possibility they moved from Pennsylvania.

Most of the services where I can search censuses indexes (Ancestry.com, Fold3, HeritageQuest.com, FamilySearch.org, etc.) allow me to define criteria to search on. I can search by last name, first and last name, age, age give or take a certain number of years (usually + or - 1, 2, 5 or 10 years) and a number of other criteria.

Doing a nationwide search for a William or William H. Cunningham, age 40 (give or take five years) with a wife named Amanda, I discover the following family living in Lincoln Township, Crawford County, Kansas:

| Cunningham, William H., | age 43 |
| Amanda, | age 35 |
| Lovena B., | age 12 |
| Rachel J., | age 10 |
| George E., | age 8 |
| Maggie, | age 6 |
| William E., | age 4 |
| John, | age 1 |

If you cannot find the family under the father's name, try the mother or one of the children.

Given the names I know belong to this family, I feel certain I have located the correct family. The ages for William and Amanda are closer, but still off – given their birthdays and the enumeration date (1 June) for the 1870 census, William should be 42 and Amanda should be 36. Most of the children's ages are just a little off, based on the 1860 census and the information I have for them. Again, a caution to look elsewhere for correct birthdates. Note also that Sarah Lovina Belle, who was listed as Sarah L. B. in the 1860 census, is now listed as Lovena B. I also note the appearance of William E. Cunningham – age 4 in the 1870 census. He is my great grandfather. His birthday was in December 1865, so his age is correctly listed in the 1870 census.

As you can see, as you work with censuses, you need to be open to errors that may have crept in. But given all their weaknesses, censuses are still a powerful resource to use for genealogical research, especially for the last 160 years or so.

# 5. STATE CENSUSES

**State & Territorial Censuses**

As helpful as the United States censuses are, many of the states (and territories before statehood) conducted their own censuses. Often overlooked, these censuses provide yet another source for locating ancestors – seeing if they remained in the area they had been in during the US Census, identifying children who may not have been born at the time of the federal census, etc., etc.

Like their elder brethren of the federal variety, some of the same pitfalls need to be remembered about state censuses: misspellings, inaccurate dates and other information may be present in state censuses. Just be careful and use them for the information they do provide.

The state and territorial censuses generally did not follow the federal practice of enumeration in the first year of each decade. The state enumerations were generally enumerated later in the decade. Some states conducted censuses frequently (in this regard, you're lucky if your ancestors lived in Michigan, New Jersey or New York, for example), and others only once (my home state of Colorado, for example). Some didn't do them at all, especially those who entered the union later than others. Sometimes these censuses were very similar in content to the US census, sometimes they were more extensive (New Jersey and New York, for example), and other times they were much more abbreviated. Regardless, these oft-forgotten records are another source of genealogical information that may help you locate and/or pin down some elusive ancestors.

> Many states conducted state censuses in addition to federal censuses.

For those states that didn't conduct censuses, some conducted "censuses" of tax payers, and while these tax lists don't list families, they do list heads of household on a specific date at a specific place, and can serve as a substitute for a state census and are therefore also a valid research tool to use. For example, say you have found your ancestor in the 1880 census. Being a keen and experienced genealogist, you know that the vast majority of the 1890 census was destroyed by fire, so you look for your ancestor in the 1900 census, but even though you find his family, he's not there. Now – that represents a pretty wide span of time in which he could have died – 20 years. But if the state has a tax list for any of the years in between 1880 and 1900, you may be able to narrow the timeframe. If, for example, he shows up in 1893, then the timeframe is down to seven years. If, however, you find his wife listed as the head of household in 1885, then the timeframe is five years. (Caution – it is possible that he may have simply abandoned his family, or divorced, or was working out of town / state, and that accounts for his disappearance!)

When states and territories conducted state censuses, they generally did so in the fifth year of the decade – 1865, 1875, 1885, 1895, etc.

In the last chapter, you may recall we followed the William Huston Cunningham family from the 1860 through 1930 censuses. They started keeping house in Pennsylvania in the late 1850s, but sometime between 1860 and the time of the 1870 census they pulled up stakes and moved to Kansas. We were fortunate enough to find them in a US census in their new state. But had that effort failed, all would not have been lost. The state they moved to – Kansas – conducted a state census in the fifth year of each decade from 1865 to 1925. Below is the information from the 1875 Kansas state census for Lincoln Township, Crawford County, Kansas on 1 March 1875:

- W. Cunningham         age 49
- A. Cunningham         age 43
- S. L. B. Cunningham   age 18
- R. J. Cunningham      age 16
- G. E. Cunningham      age 14
- M. E. Cunningham      age 12

- W. E. Cunningham     age 10
- J. F. Cunningham     age 4
- E. J. Cunningham     age 1

The 1875 Kansas state census only included the initials of each person, but we know enough about this family (names and ages) to identify it as the William Huston and Amanda Cunningham family. Even though it only listed initials for each individual, it asked a number of helpful questions. It asked the place of birth (all were born in Pennsylvania except Effie – E. J. – who was born in Kansas) and asked a wonderful question:

> *Where from to Kansas – meaning state or territory of US, or country if a foreigner?*

That last question is a delicious tidbit of information that might assist a genealogist in finding more information on a particular family. Using this state census, I can narrow the timeframe that this family left Pennsylvania. Not only do we know they were in Kansas on 1 March 1875, we also know their 1-year-old daughter Effie was born in Kansas – so our timeframe is now narrowed from the ten years between US censuses, to about four years – between 1870 (US census) and 1874 (Effie's birth in Kansas). Other records – such as land records or newspaper articles for the area, my help us pinpoint this family's arrival even more closely.

Each state's census varies from the censuses for other states and territories, and often varies from year to year. But when you can find these censuses, they can prove to be very helpful and provide another snapshot of your ancestors at a specific point in time.

I have used several books to assist me in locating state census records:

- *State Census Records,* Lainhart, Ann S. (Baltimore Genealogical Publishing Co, 1992). Ann Lainhart's book is specifically devoted to state censuses and has been a great assist to me in my genealogy research.

- *Red Book: American State, County & Town Sources*, Alice Eichholz (editor), (Ancestry Publishing, June 1, 2004). The *Red Book* is a great book to have handy, and among other information, provides state-by-state information on where to go to find information on censuses.

Ms. Lainhart's book isn't very expensive, but the *Red Book* is. I have found the *Red Book* in the reference section of my local library.

In addition to these sources, I have also found Google to be an effective tool in locating information about state census records. Just Google *(State) state census* (for example: *Colorado state census*) and you should get some good information. Also, I stumbled across this great website a few years ago: *www.newhorizonsgenealogical services.com/*. They do a nice job of listing what census records can be found on a state-by-state basis.

Ancestry.com, HeritageQuest.com, Fold3 and FamilySearch.org also offer many of the state censuses online.

# 6. MORTALITY SCHEDULES

Another important yet oft-overlooked set of records that were kept coincident with the US census were the **Mortality Schedules** for the 1850 through 1880 censuses. These schedules listed everyone who had died between June 1 of the year before the census and May 31 of the census year (1 June 1859 through 31 May 1860, for example). They listed the name, age, sex, marital status, race, occupation, birth place, cause of death and length of illness for each individual who passed away during that year.

Now, one year's worth of death information might not seem like a lot, but it represents 10% of the deaths in a decade, so you have the possibility of finding death information about that elusive ancestor of yours. And – this before most states began requiring that deaths be recorded. The mortality schedule may in fact be the only place the death is recorded.

Let me give you a simple example using a member of my family. I know that many generations of my family were born, lived and died in Scott County, Virginia. Using the mortality schedule of the 1880 US census, I searched for any Quillens in Scott County Virginia that might have died between June 1, 1879 and May 31, 1880. Sure enough, I found this listing in the mortality schedule:

• James G. Quillin    1/12    Male    White    Month of death – January

I then searched to see if I could find the family to whom he belonged, and discovered this sad family:

• Ewell H. Quillin          40        Male          White
• Elizabeth D. Quillin     40        Female        White

As heartbroken as Ewell and Elizabeth were at the loss of their precious one-month-old son James G., I believe they would have been doubly heartbroken not to have their little son with them, gathered together as a family in my records. Had I not checked the mortality schedule for 1880, I would likely have never known that James was a member of their family, because his name appeared in no other source that I have yet found. I would have missed this important family member.

Checking the mortality schedules and matching those you find there to their family is fairly straight forward. Here's how I found James G. Quillin, and was able to join him to his family:

1. I used my subscription to Ancestry.com to access the 1880 census. (I was unable to get this information through *Familysearch.org*; perhaps it is there, but I could not find it!)

2. I searched for the mortality schedule for 1880 using Quillen and Scott County, Virginia as delineators.

3. I found James G. Quillin (note the different spelling) listed on the mortality schedule in the Estilville, Scott County, Virginia enumeration district. I noted that he was associated with family #104 of the enumeration district.

4. I then went to the 1880 US Census (not the mortality schedule) for the Estilville, Scott County, Virginia enumeration district and found family #104 in the enumeration district – Ewell H. and Elizabeth D. Quillin.

**Note:** the census enumerators numbered each dwelling and family they found in each enumeration district. These numbers are the left-most columns on the census record. In this manner, I was able to match young James with his family.

You'll find each state's mortality schedules wherever you find their federal censuses. Those locations include each state's library and archives, several subscription-based services like Ancestry.com, Heritage Quest, etc., and at the Family History Library of the LDS Church. And don't forget to check the records or websites of genealogy societies in the area where you are doing your genealogical research.

Following is a synopsis of which years mortality schedules were kept by state:

**Alabama** — Mortality schedules exist for the 1850, 1860, 1870, and 1880 censuses.

**Alaska** — Mortality schedules do not exist for Alaska.

**Arizona** — Mortality schedules exist for the 1850, 1860, 1870, and 1880 censuses.

**Arkansas** — Mortality schedules exist for the 1870 and 1880 censuses.

**California** — Mortality schedules exist for the 1850, 1860, 1870, and 1880 censuses.

**Colorado** — Mortality schedules exist for the 1860, 1870, and 1880 censuses. There is also a mortality schedule associated with a special interim census conducted in Colorado in 1885.

**Connecticut** — Mortality schedules exist for the 1850, 1860, 1870, and 1880 censuses.

**Delaware** — Mortality schedules exist for the 1850, 1860, 1870, and 1880 censuses.

**District of Columbia** — Mortality schedules exist for the 1850, 1860, 1870, and 1880 censuses.

**Florida** — Mortality schedules exist for the 1850, 1860, 1870, and 1880 censuses. There is also a mortality schedule associated with a special interim census conducted in Florida in 1885.

**Georgia** — Mortality schedules exist for the 1850, 1860, 1870, and 1880 censuses.

**Hawaii** — There are no mortality schedules available for Hawaii.

**Idaho** — Mortality schedules exist for the 1870 and 1880 censuses.

**Illinois** — Mortality schedules exist for the 1850, 1860, 1870, and 1880 censuses.

**Indiana** — Mortality schedules exist for the 1850, 1860, 1870, and 1880 censuses.

**Iowa** — Mortality schedules exist for the 1850, 1860, 1870, and 1880 censuses.

**Kansas** — Mortality schedules exist for the 1860, 1870, and 1880 censuses.

**Kentucky** — Mortality schedules exist for the 1850, 1860, 1870, and 1880 censuses.

**Louisiana** — Mortality schedules exist for the 1850, 1860, 1870, and 1880 censuses.

**Maine** — Mortality schedules exist for the 1850, 1860, 1870, and 1880 censuses.

**Maryland** — Mortality schedules exist for the 1850, 1860, 1870, and 1880 censuses.

**Massachusetts** — Mortality schedules exist for the 1850, 1860, 1870, and 1880 censuses.

**Michigan** — Mortality schedules exist for the 1850, 1860, 1870, and 1880 censuses.

**Minnesota** — Mortality schedules exist for the 1850, 1860 and 1870 censuses.

**Mississippi** — Mortality schedules exist for the 1850, 1860, 1870, and 1880 censuses.

**Missouri** — Mortality schedules exist for the 1850, 1860, 1870, and 1880 censuses.

**Montana** — Mortality schedules exist for the 1860 and 1870 censuses.

**Nebraska** — Mortality schedules exist for the 1860, 1870, and 1880 censuses. There is also a mortality schedule associated with a special interim census conducted in 1885.

**Nevada** — Mortality schedules exist for the 1860 and 1870 censuses.

**New Hampshire** — Mortality schedules exist for the 1850, 1860, 1870, and 1880 censuses.

**New Jersey** — Mortality schedules exist for the 1850, 1860, 1870, and 1880 censuses.

**New Mexico** — Mortality schedules exist for the 1850, 1860, and 1870 censuses. There is also a mortality schedule associated with a special interim census conducted in New Mexico in 1885.

**New York** — Mortality schedules exist for the 1850, 1860, 1870, and 1880 censuses.

**North Carolina** — Mortality schedules exist for the 1850, 1860, 1870, and 1880 censuses. There is also a mortality schedule associated with a special interim census conducted in North Carolina in 1885.

**North Dakota** — Mortality schedules exist for the 1860, 1870 and 1880 censuses. There is also a mortality schedule associated with a special interim census conducted in North Dakota in 1885.

**Ohio** — Mortality schedules exist for the 1850, 1860 and 1880 censuses.

**Oklahoma** — Oklahoma had no mortality schedules.

**Oregon** — Mortality schedules exist for the 1850, 1860, 1870, and 1880 censuses.

**Pennsylvania** — Mortality schedules exist for the 1850, 1860, 1870, and 1880 censuses.

**Rhode Island** — Mortality schedules exist for the 1850, 1860, 1870, and 1880 censuses.

**South Carolina** — Mortality schedules exist for the 1870 census.

**South Dakota** — Mortality schedules exist for the 1860, 1870, and 1880 censuses. There is also a mortality schedule associated with a special interim census conducted in South Dakota in 1885.

**Tennessee** — Mortality schedules exist for the 1850, 1860,1870, and 1880 censuses.

**Texas** — Mortality schedules exist for the 1850, 1860, 1870, and 1880 censuses.

**Utah** — Mortality schedules exist for the 1850, 1860, 1870, and 1880 censuses.

**Vermont** — Mortality schedules exist for the 1850, 1860, 1870, and 1880 censuses.

**Virginia** — Mortality schedules exist for the 1850, 1860, 1870, and 1880 censuses.

**Washington** — Mortality schedules exist for the 1860, 1870, and 1880 censuses.

**West Virginia** — Mortality schedules exist for the 1850, 1860, 1870, and 1880 censuses.

**Wisconsin** — Mortality schedules exist for the 1850, 1860, 1870, and 1880 censuses.

**Wyoming** — Mortality schedules exist for the 1870 and 1880 censuses.

As of this writing, only about 15% to 20% of the mortality schedules listed above have been indexed. However, the censuses through 1940 have been indexed, so you can find their family members, and then check the mortality schedule for that enumeration district. While not perfect, that's one way to do it. Consider, for example, a mother or father who had been living with their married daughter. If you didn't know their daughter's married name or where she and her family were living, you may not be able to locate them if they are not in a mortality schedule that is indexed. Otherwise, you're limited to searching through all the

> Mortality Schedules are valuable research sources for identifying the death dates of some ancestors.

mortality schedules for the places your ancestor had been living. If they moved since the last census (where you learned the township, county and state where your ancestor lived), they may be lost to you until mortality schedules are indexed. Indexing mortality schedules is a frequent activity undertaken by genealogy societies.

Mortality schedules are available through Ancestry.com, HeritageQuest, Fold3 FamilySearch.org, the Daughters of the American Revolution organization, and the state archives of the various states. Additionally, bear in mind that quite a few free websites have popped up in recent years that also offer access to mortality schedules. While their collections aren't usually as extensive as some of the subscription services, they are free, so you may want to try them out first. Several I have found helpful include Mortality Schedules.com at *www.mortalityschedules.com* and New Horizons Genealogy at *www.newhorizonsgenealogicalservices.com*. As new sites are added all the time, just Google *Mortality Schedules* and see what comes up.

Note: the most complete set of Mortality Schedules I have found are at Ancestry.com. Here is the URL for them. You can find them (at least as of this writing) at *search.ancestry.com/search/db.aspx?dbid=8756*. If that URL doesn't work, you can try to figure out how to find it at Ancestry, or simply Google *Mortality Schedules Ancestry.com*.

Don't overlook Mortality Schedules!

# 7. OTHER CENSUS SCHEDULES

Regarding censuses, we have discussed federal censuses, state censuses and mortality schedules. In addition to these censuses, there are a number of other census-style records / schedules enumerated at both the state and federal level that may shed some light on some of your tough-to-find ancestors. Following are some of the more common of these uncommon schedules, and a little about them.

## Slave Schedules

When I first learned about slave schedules, I got very excited, thinking these would be a welcome tool for genealogists doing research on African Americans. Alas, the slave schedules turned out to be nothing more than tally marks categorizing slaves as male, female and their ages, much akin to the US censuses prior to 1840. On the next page you'll find a partial transcription of a slave schedule from Kentucky.

Separate slave schedules were enumerated during the 1850 and 1860 censuses. Prior to that, they were included in the tally of the slave owner's family. The 1840 census for Henry Clay of Bourbon County, Kentucky shows a family of three adults (one apparently a mother or mother-in-law), four children and 47 slaves of varying ages and sexes.

In the 1850 and 1860 slave schedules, slaves are listed under the slave owner's name, but a notation indicates whether they were in the employ of another individual. But still, these listings provide only the slave owner's name and the name of the individual who rented the slave from the owner.

There are a few – a very few – times when slaves were in fact named. For the 1850 and 1860 censuses, enumerators were instructed to list the names of slaves who

### Sample Slave Schedule

US 1860 slave schedule for the Eastern District, Bourbon County, Kentucky for Henry Clay:

| Age | Gender | Race |
| --- | --- | --- |
| 87 | Female | Black |
| 71 | Male | Black |
| 65 | Male | Black |
| 60 | Female | Black |
| 46 | Female | Black |
| 45 | Male | Black |
| 36 | Male | Black |
| 31 | Male | Black |
| 30 | Male | Mulato |
| 30 | Female | Black |
| 28 | Male | Mulatto |

Slave schedules also asked whether the slave had been manumitted (freed / emancipated) or whether the slave was a fugitive from the state. It also asked for the number of slave houses in existence.

were over 100 years old. That happened seldom, of course, but it did happen. In reviewing slave schedules, I have run across slaves reported to be as old as 125 years old! Which brings me to another point – the ages listed for slaves are generally considered to be notoriously wrong. (But can you for a moment imagine the things this woman experienced in her 125-ish years of life! I found her in the 1860 census, so her birth date would be approximately 1735, meaning she was a woman approaching middle age during the Revolutionary War. And she lived to see the Civil War – quite a span of experiences / years!)

Occasionally, whenever entire plantations were enumerated, the names of all the slaves on the plantation were included in the schedules. These times were sporadic at best, but worth checking out if you have an ancestor that worked on a large plantation.

**Military Veterans Schedules**
The 1840 and 1890 federal censuses included schedules that enumerated Revolutionary War and War of 1812 veterans (1840) and veterans of the Civil War and Mexican War (1890).

Slave schedules tended to be tally sheets only. But do check them – just in case!

As we discussed earlier in this book, the US censuses through 1840 did not provide the names of anyone beyond the head of the household. Everyone else in the household – including slaves – were merely counted by tally marks indicating age range and gender. However, the 1840 US census did provide the names of Revolutionary War and War of 1812 veterans or their widows.

While the main enumeration pages for the 1840 census just listed the tallies, the back pages of the census were reserved for information about veterans or their widows. (To find the back page, simply go to the next page of the census.) A column on the back page was titled:

*Pensioners for Revolutionary
or military services, included
in the foregoing*

Under that heading was the word *Names,* along with another column for the age of the veteran or widow. Scanning numerous 1840 censuses, I did not find the names of many veterans or their widows, but I did find a few.

So the 1840 census provides the names of veterans or their widows, their age and their residence – helpful clues for finding your ancestors. If you find your ancestor's name listed as a veteran or widow in the 1840 census, then you'll want to search for military records for them, which may shed additional light on their lives.

While doing research for this book, I ran across a wonderful website hosted by Kathy Leigh. Kathy has transcribed all the pensioners listed in the 1840 census. The information is available by state and county, and lists the pensioner's name, age and the head of the household where the pensioner was living. It also provides the town, county and state where the pensioner lived. The list is searchable by name, or you can just scan the various states for which the information is included. The website, called *The 1840 Census of Pensioners, Revolutionary and Military Services* can be found at *www.us-roots.org/colonialamerica/census/1840/index.html.* I do not know if Kathy compiled all the information herself or if she had help, but it must have been a huge project, and I appreciate her efforts. The website is part of the Colonial America website. As I scanned one state's information, it appeared that about one in three of these octogenarian and septuagenarian veterans were living with family members.

The 1890 veterans schedule captured information on the service provided by veterans. It included the names of "Surviving soldiers, sailors, mariners and widows," rank, company, regiment or vessel, date of enlistment and date of discharge, and length of service calculated in years, months and days. It also listed the veteran's post office address, any disabilities he may have had, and a column for remarks.

About now you're probably thinking I am out of my ever-lovin' mind, since any genealogist worth his or her salt knows that all but mere fragments of the 1890 US census was lost. So how can we be talking about a veteran's schedule from the 1890 census? While it is true most of the 1890 census was lost, most of the veteran's schedules were not. 1890 veteran schedules are available for about 34 states, the District of Columbia, Indian territories and naval yards and ships. States for which 1890 veterans schedules **do not** exist are: Alabama, Alaska, Arizona, Arkansas, California, Colorado, Connecticut, Delaware, Florida, Georgia, Hawaii, Idaho, Iowa, Illinois, Indiana and Kansas. Portions of the Kentucky and Louisiana schedules are also missing.

The 1910 census asked if individuals were survivors of the Union or Confederate Army or Navy – a helpful clue that may lead you to more records (see the chapter on Military Records).

*Veteran's schedules are valuable in finding my military ancestors.*

**Special Interim Census – 1885**

The special interim census of 1885 was mentioned briefly in the state censuses and mortality schedules chapters of this book. The federal government funded this effort for a handful of states: Colorado, Florida, Nebraska and North and South Dakota territories as well as New Mexico Territory. It asked essentially the same questions as the 1880 census used for the rest of the United States. Here are the questions:

**1885 — Enumeration date 1 June, 1885**
• Name
• Color
• Sex
• Age June 1 in census year
• Relationship to head of house
• Single
• Married
• Widowed
• Divorced
• Married in census year
• Occupation
• Other information
• Can't read or write
• Place of birth
• Place of birth of father
• Place of birth of mother
• Enumeration date

If your ancestors lived in one of those states or territories in 1885, be sure and check out this oft-overlooked census. It is especially important when considering that the vast majority of the 1890 census was lost in a fire. Other states go from the 1880 census to the 1900 census – a twenty-year gap. Consider your own family and the changes that have taken place over the last two decades, and you begin to see the magnitude of the loss of the 1890 census. The 1885 census, along with some state censuses, help bridge that lengthy gap.

**American Indian Census Rolls**

These special schedules of the US census for the years 1885 through 1940 are helpful to those seeking their Native American ancestors. Ancestry.com has these censuses available at *search.ancestry.com/search/db.aspx?dbid=1059*. Included in the censuses are the individual's Indian name, his or her English name, their age, gender and relation to the head of the household. Following is a transcription of an Indian Schedule from the 1930 US census for the Pine Ridge Reservation in South Dakota:

| | Sample Indian Schedule | | | |
|---|---|---|---|---|
| **Indian Name** | **English Name** | **Sex** | **Relation** | **Age** |
| Mato Hunkasni | Slow Bear | M | Head | 51 |
| Sunkgka Ota Vin | Plenty White Horse | F | Wife | 50 |
| Kiciza | Frank Fight | M | Nephew | 27 |
| Aiyapi | Talks About | F | Daughter | 24 |
| Mato Hunkasni | John Slow Bear | M | Son | 18 |
| Iyar Payapi | Grabs Him | M | Son | 17 |
| Kokipesni | Not Afraid | M | Son | 10 |

The census record indicates that this enumeration is for the Pine Ridge Agency Indian Reservation in South Dakota, and consists primarily of Sioux and Cheyenne.

**Deaf Couples**

Here's an exceptionally little-known tidbit of genealogical trivia: In the 1880 census, the federal government was curious about its deaf citizens. Whenever an enumerator ran across a husband and/or wife who were deaf, they were asked to complete a special four-page form and send it in to the government. These were gathered and studied by the government as well as the Volta Laboratory and Bureau, the brainchild of Alexander Graham Bell (whose wife had been deaf since early childhood). The extra pages they completed contained a tremendous amount of genealogical information not found in the 1880 census standard set of questions, and may prove helpful for genealogists. Here are the questions asked:

- Names of husband and wife
- Date and place of marriage
- Whether parties were related prior to marriage, and if so, what was the relationship
- Total number of children
- How many of the children were deaf
- Names and birthdates of children
- Death dates of children, if applicable
- Husband's father's and mother's names (including mother's maiden name)
- Wife's father's and mother's names (including mother's maiden name)
- Death dates of husband's and wife's parents
- Ages of husband's and wife's parents when they died
- Siblings of the husband, including their birth dates
- How many of the husband's siblings were deaf
- Siblings of wife, including their birth dates
- How many of the wife's siblings were deaf

Wow. If one of your ancestors was deaf and completed such a form, you will likely add a great deal to the genealogical information you have about that family for at least three generations! Among other places, you can find these gems at Ancestry.com at *search.ancestry.com/search/db.aspx?dbid=1582*.

## Defective, Dependent, and Delinquent Schedules

If an individual was listed in the 1880 census as being "Defective, Dependent or Delinquent," that person was included in a supplemental schedule. Individuals were categorized into the following categories:

- Insane
- Idiots
- Deaf mutes
- Blind
- Paupers and indigent persons
- Homeless children
- Prisoners

Most of the questions asked for each of the above categories shed precious little information of genealogical value. In fact, some of the questions are downright personal / offensive / intrusive by today's standards of privacy and decency. You can find these schedules on Ancestry.com at *search.ancestry.com/search/db.aspx?dbid=1634.*

# 8. TRICKS OF THE CENSUS TRADE

I have worked for years with censuses and found some tricks that have allowed me to find ancestors in the censuses even when it appeared they were playing very effective games of hide-and-go-seek. I will share these tricks over the course of the next few pages. If you have discovered some tricks I have not mentioned, please let me know and I may include them in future editions of this book.

**Check neighboring families**
When you find your ancestor, look at the surrounding families for familiar surnames. Be sensitive to incorrect / different spellings of names. Knowing the maiden name of your ancestor may allow you to find others of her family nearby. Remember – several generations ago, families often stayed near one another for generations.

Let me give you an example:

You may recall from the first chapter of this book that my second great grandparents were William Huston and Amanda Stunkard Cunningham. I was fortunate to find them in the 1860 census of Wells Township, Fulton County, Pennsylvania:

Cunningham, William H.  age 30
               Amanda     age 28
               Sarah L. B.  age  3
               Rachel      age  1

One of the nice things about Amanda's maiden name — Stunkard – is that it's not a common name, and anyone nearby with that surname is bound to be related.

Perhaps they are Amanda's parents, or brothers, uncles, cousins, etc. Searching nearby families, I find two families with the Stunkard surname:

| Stunkard, William | 52 | | Stunkard, James | 36 |
| --- | --- | --- | --- | --- |
| Margaret | 50 | | Matilda | 34 |
| Robert | 24 | | Susan | 11 |
| Sara | 21 | | John | 9 |
| Eliza | 19 | | William | 7 |
| Samuel | 17 | | Catharin | 5 |
| William | 15 | | Virginia | 2 |
| Martha | 13 | | | |
| Nancy | 11 | | | |
| Margret | 9 | | | |
| Martha | 4 | | | |

These two families are living in the same county and township as Amanda and William. The first couple, William and Margaret, could be Amanda's parents, as they are both the correct age to have a daughter Amanda's age (26 in 1860). Or perhaps they could be an aunt and uncle.

The other family – James and Matilda – could also be related to Amanda. James is about the age where he could be an older brother of Amanda's. Or he could be a cousin. He's too old to be a son of William and Margaret.

Most of the lines of my family lived in rural America for most of their generations, especially the generations I would use censuses to find. Once I locate a member of the family in a county, I routinely search for other family members elsewhere in the same county. I just go through the census for that county page by page.

> Check neighboring families for other family members.

### Check previous or subsequent censuses

Speaking of following threads, one way to do that is to check the census that was held ten years before, as well as ten years later, looking for clues that might tie up some loose ends. Using my previous example of Amanda Stunkard and checking ten years before in the 1850 census, I would look for a Stunkard family with a 16-year-old girl named Amanda. I'll also check for William and Margaret as well as James and Matilda. I'll check initially in the same county and state. Checking the 1850 census (remember – the 1850 census was the first to list the names of all family members), I find both those families:

| Stunkard, William | 42 | Stunkard, James | 26 |
|---|---|---|---|
| Margaret | 40 | Matilda | 24 |
| Robert | 14 | Susan | 1 |
| Sara | 11 | Robert | 24 |
| Eliza | 9 | Amanda | 16 |
| Samuel | 7 | | |
| William | 5 | | |
| Martha | 3 | | |
| Nancy | 1 | | |

I can use the children's names and ages to determine that these were the same families I found in the 1860 census. So – William and Margaret are in the same area ten years earlier, but the real find is 16-year-old Amanda living with James and Matilda, along with Robert F. My assumption at this point is that James and Robert F. are Amanda's older brothers. Also, since other searches in the county, state and nation-wide did not turn up Sarah's parents (Matthew and Sarah), I will assume they have died at this point.

While these are assumptions, I must still be open to the possibility that there are other reasons Amanda is living with James and Matilda. Perhaps she's a niece, or cousin. Perhaps her parents haven't died – maybe her parents really are William and Margaret – but she's merely moved in with James to help tend 1-year-old Susan because Matilda is ailing. Or…so many other possibilities. High on the possibility list, however, is that Amanda is living with her brother's family.

See if I can find my ancestor as a child in an earlier census to identify her family.

**Be aware of places of birth**

The 1880 census was the first to ask for the birth places of the parents as well as the individual. This is helpful as you try to match up families. For example, earlier I surmised that James M., Robert F. and Amanda Stunkard were siblings, since I found Robert F. and Amanda living with James M. If I can find these individuals in the 1880 census and see if they list their parents as being born in the same place, then I have one more piece of data tying them together.

Using these three potential siblings as an example, I search for them in the 1880 census. Without listing the rest of the family members, here's what I found for each: James M. – no James M. He disappeared after the 1860 census...I surmise he has passed away.

Robert F. 54, born in Pennsylvania, father born in Pennsylvania, mother born in Pennsylvania

Amanda 46, born in Pennsylvania, father born in Pennsylvania, mother born in Pennsylvania

This information lends credence to my earlier assumption that Amanda and Robert F. may be siblings. James is a mystery that will have to be solved by other research.

**Be aware of other names listed with families**

As you research the censuses, be aware of other individuals listed with your family, as they may provide you clues about your ancestors. For example, the 1870 census of Fulton County, Pennsylvania lists this family:

Lambertsen, C.A.   31
      Jessie M.  30
Julia Cunningham  75

If I were doing research on the Lambertsen family and ran across this entry, I might make the assumption that the 75-year-old woman living with the family was

Jessie's mother, and therefore Jessie's maiden name was Cunningham. While we won't know that with 100% certainty, it is another piece of the ancestral puzzle that may fit nicely. Other possibilities include: Julia is a neighbor or friend, Julia remarried and her current surname isn't Jessie's maiden name, etc. With 45 years between their ages, it's even conceivable that Julia is Jessie's grandmother. But – it gives me something to look for – a marriage certificate or record in which a C. A. Lambertsen married Jessie Cunningham.

Beginning with the 1880 census, each census asked for the relationship of each listed individual to the head of household. Prior to that – in the 1850, 1860 and 1870 censuses, you need to look for clues such as just described.

### Use all family members
This has been an especially successful tactic for me to use when an entire family drops out of sight between censuses. It works whether you are checking a previous census, or a subsequent census. It has been particularly effective in finding families where the names have been misspelled. Just a few months prior to writing this book, I used this tactic to find my third and fourth great grandparents in the census. In both cases, their surnames had been misspelled, so that when I searched for the families in indexes, they did not appear. Instead of searching for a Quillen family, I instead searched using only the first name of my second great grandfather, Jonathan Quillen. When I did that, I found two families I had been unable to find for years! I went to the 1860 census for Lee County, Virginia, and searched for Jonathan, and here's what I got:

Qulline, Frank    30
      Susannah  30
      Johnathan  12
      Martin    10

And as an added bonus, living immediately next door were my fourth great grandparents:

Quilling, Leven  70

| | |
|---|---|
| Sillas | 66 |
| Henry | 18 |
| Salina | 17 |
| Ruthy | 16 |
| Savina | 21 |

Note that the surnames for both families were misspelled – Qulline and Quilling and so never came up when I searched indexes. Even though they misspelled Jonathan (Johnathan) on the census, it was close enough for me to come up as a hit. This is an especially effective tactic if one of the members of the family has an odd / peculiar / distinctive name. Earlier, one of my examples included a family named Matilda, a different enough name to help me find the family when they suddenly disappear.

**Use what you already know**
An effective tool for searching the censuses and identifying the correct families is to use the information you already have. I am fortunate to have information from the center section of our family Bible for a number of my family lines. Earlier, I used an example of my second great grandparents, William Huston and Amanda Stunkard Cunningham. As I was researching censuses, I found a family to which Amanda could have belonged as a daughter:

| | |
|---|---|
| Stunkard, William | 52 |
| Margaret | 50 |
| Robert | 24 |
| Sara | 21 |
| Eliza | 19 |
| Samuel | 17 |
| William | 15 |
| Martha | 13 |
| Nancy | 11 |
| Margret | 9 |
| Martha | 4 |
| Margaret McCashen | 15 |

In my earlier example, I mentioned it might be possible that this couple could be the parents of 26-year-old Amanda. Even though the family Bible said Amanda's parents were Matthew and Margaret, I should still be open to the possibility that the father's name was William and not Matthew, or perhaps it was William Matthew and he went by William. But I also happen to know (from our family Bible) that some of Amanda's siblings are McClelland, John, Furgeson and Margaret. And none of William and Margaret Stunkard's children shared those names, so I can reasonably assume this is not Amanda's immediate family.

### Use wild cards....

When you are searching indexes for your ancestors, some of the services (Ancestry.com, Fold3 and FamilySearch.org) allow you to use wild cards in place of letters as you search for names. So, if I am having trouble finding an ancestor that I just know should be in the census (for example – the family is in the 1860 census and the 1880 census, but seemingly missing from the 1870 census), I might use wild cards in the spelling of their name. So instead of searching for Quillen, I can look for Qui***n. That covers Quillen, Quillan, Quillon, Quinlan, etc. This is an effective tool to use if an ancestor's name was misspelled in the census, or the indexer misinterpreted what was written on the census.

### Advanced Search

Most of the subscription and free services you use to search census indexes allow you to do a brief search – surname, age and place of birth, for example. They all also offer advanced search capabilities, where you can really refine your request. This is especially nice if many people share your ancestor's surname (Smith, Jones, Johnson, etc.) in the area you area searching. Some of the options include:

> Using wild cards will help you find families whose names have been misspelled.

• First name
• Middle name
• Surname
• Place of birth

• Year of birth (+ or – 1, 2, 5, 10 and even 20 years)
• Place of residence
• Family members' names (spouse, child, parents, siblings)

These advanced searches can narrow down the results of your search tremendously. But a caution: if you narrow your search too much, you may eliminate your ancestor because of poor information, misspellings, estimated birth dates that were wrong, etc. So if you use the advanced search capability and don't find your ancestor, don't worry. Just step back a bit and use fewer criteria.

## Use the neighbors

This is a tactic I have used to find an ancestor who I just knew was still in the area where they had been. When they disappear, perhaps you can use a neighbor. Here's how: In the census where you found your ancestor, pick a neighboring family. See if you can find that neighboring family in the previous (or subsequent) census. If you find the neighbor, look around him to see if your family is nearby.

# 9. MILITARY RECORDS – AN OVERVIEW

In the vernacular of my teenagers: "Oh. My. Goodness." That pretty well sums up my feelings about military records – they are an abundant source of genealogical information and they are far too often overlooked by genealogists.

Through the years I have sought for ancestors here and there. Sometimes my efforts have yielded great gobs of information, and sometimes I come up empty. As often as not, when I find a lot of information in one place, it is usually in a military record, or a series of records for a veteran ancestor. Following is the genealogical information I have found in military records:

- Birth date
- Birth place
- Marriage date and place
- Death date
- Wife's maiden name
- Wife's birth date and place
- Wife's death date
- Ages of all children 16 years of age and younger
- Place of residence

All that from various military records! In addition, although not genealogical in nature, I found the following, which helped make my ancestors seem more alive to me:

- Physical description: height, weight, hair and eye color, etc.
- Occupation(s)

- The amount of pension he or his wife received
- His rank, branch of service, company, regiment, etc.
- Battles he fought in
- Pay stubs
- Roll calls
- Letters of commendation
- Promotion information
- Details of his injuries and death

Hopefully by this point you are convinced of the value of military records for researching your ancestors, and you may ask, "Where do I find these wonderful records?" Let me set the stage (battlefield?) a little better first, and then we'll get into where to find these records.

> Military records contain a lot of genealogical information.

**American Wars**

The history of our nation is a history of wars. Whether for expansion of the union, preservation of the union, the protection of our worldwide interests or the protection of our allies and the downtrodden, Americans have fought in many wars. If you are not sure whether one of your ancestors fought, see if they were of military age (roughly 16 to 40 years of age) during any of these wars:

- King Philip's War (1675-1676)
- King William's War (1689-1697)
- Queen Anne's War (1702-1713)
- French and Indian Wars (1754 to 1763)
- Revolutionary War (1775 to 1783)
- War of 1812 (1812 to 1815)
- Blackhawk War (1832)
- Mexican-American War (1846 to 1848)
- Civil War (1861 to 1865)
- Spanish-American War (1898)

- Philippine War (1899 to 1902)
- World War I (1917 to 1918)
- World War II (1941 to 1945)
- Korean Conflict (1950 to 1953)
- Vietnam War (1965 to 1973)
- Gulf War / Desert Storm (1991 to 1992)
- Gulf War / War on Terror / Iraq / Afghanistan (2003 — ?)

It seems that if you had ancestors born between about 1750 and present day, there would have been a war they could have been involved in. If you had male ancestors that were of military age during any of those wars, it may well be worth your time to check out military records for genealogical information. Each of the wars / conflicts the United States was involved in generated varying amounts of records that may prove helpful in your hunt for information about your ancestors.

The information available is bookended at each end of the timeline by:

• Less and / or lost information in the earlier wars (pre-Civil War), and
• Privacy laws that kick in around the World War II era

But in between, there is a rich amount of information available on ancestors who fought in America's wars. Information from the Civil War is especially abundant. There is more information available for Union soldiers and less for Confederate soldiers, but still a great deal of information is available.

**Where to Begin**
If you know that you had an ancestor who fought in one of America's wars – family tradition, a picture of him in military uniform, etc., then you might go right to the military records that deal with the war he was in. When beginning your search, use common sense. If you are trying to find information from military records about an ancestor that was born in 1855, you probably won't find him listed in enlistment or service records during the Civil War! (However, you may find him mentioned in a pension application by his father or his widowed mother — more on that later.)

Believe it or not, one of the most powerful tools for finding information about ancestors who may have served in one of America's wars is that great search engine *Google*. I have found many military records by simply Googling the name of my ancestor, followed by the war I thought he may have served in.

For example, I have a pretty good idea that my third great grandfather, Leonidas Horney, served in the military, since I have an old photograph of him dressed in a military uniform. Since he was born in 1817, I reasoned he may have served in the Blackhawk War (1832), Mexican-American War (1846 to 1848) or the Civil War (1861 to 1865).

I Googled *Leonidas Horney Blackhawk War* and got a number of hits. None of them showed him as being in the army during the Blackhawk War, but one of the hits listed him as a private in Company E of the Illinois Foot Volunteers during the Mexican War, assigned to Captain Mear's company.

As a bonus, however, my search for *Leonidas Horney Blackhawk War* yielded some information about his father, Samuel Horney, who served in the Blackhawk War when he was 44 years old. A link also took me to a photo of the old gentleman, along with a link to a compiled biography about him.

The picture I have of Leonidas in a military uniform shows a middle-aged man, not one in his 30s, so I thought I should also check to see if there were any records that showed he had served during the Civil War. So I Googled *Leonidas Horney Civil War*. The first hit to greet me was an extensive article on him, including his obituary. The article provided details about his military service – that although he was older than the age of enlistment at the outbreak of the war, he enlisted anyway. It said that although he opposed the administration (which I thought was interesting, since he lived about 60 miles from Springfield, where Abraham Lincoln was from), he joined to "crush the traitors." It also provided me with a very important piece of information about his service:

> Initially, Leonidas had planned to enlist in his home state of
> Illinois but, due to the vast number of volunteers already

enlisted, he traveled to St. Louis and joined Co. A, 10th Missouri Infantry.

This last point – Leonidas's service in the 10th Missouri Infantry – was an important step in my genealogical research for this ancestor – the nation's military records are kept by unit. With that information in hand, I Googled *Missouri Civil War Records*. I received over five million hits, and selected one of the first ones: *Index to the Civil War in Missouri*. Once I got to the website, one of the options was *Index to Officers in Missouri Military Units*. I selected that, and within seconds had the following information:

> Leonidas Horney, original commission:
>
> Captain, 10th Missouri Infantry
>
> Subsequent promotions:
>
> Major 10th Missouri Infantry
>
> Lieutenant Colonel 10th Missouri Infantry

So as you search for your armed ancestor, beginning with Google (or Yahoo! Or Bing, etc.) is a great idea. Those search engines or others may provide you with important clues to finding the military records of your ancestors. And one of the most important clues is his branch of service (army, navy, marines, coast guard, etc.) and military unit.

Armed with your ancestor's name and military unit, it's time to move a step forward to learning more about this gallant forebear of yours. There are a number of routes you can take, but all lead to the National Archives.

> To get his records, I need to find my ancestor's military unit.

### The National Archives

With the power of the Internet (and the efforts of countless volunteer genealogists and genealogical entrepreneurs), more and more military records are finding their way online. Regardless of the record, all of them have one thing in common – they all originated at one time or another with the National Archives, the repository of the nation's military records. The website for NARA (National Archives and Records Administration) is *www.archives.gov*. Learning to leverage the information available from or through the National Archives will be a great advantage to you in your search for your military ancestors. The National Archives has the following military records available for research:

- Volunteer military service
- US Army military records
- US Navy records
- US Marine Corps
- US Coast Guard and its predecessors (Revenue Cutter, Life Saving Services, and Bureau of Lighthouses)
- Civil War Service and pension records

As you can imagine, the number of military records held in the National Archives is tremendous. Many of them are still in paper form. Many more are microfilmed. Some are being digitized and are available online from the National Archives, but at this point, precious few of NARA's records are available online through their website. Fortunately, realizing the great demand and their limited ability to digitize their records themselves, NARA has entered into agreement with various subscription services (most notably Fold3 and Ancestry.com) to begin digitizing their military collections. As of this writing, a very small percentage of military records are online but Fold3 and Ancestry.com are working feverishly to change that.

If you cannot find the records you want online, from NARA or one of her subscription service providers, you may request copies of records or view them in person. To request military records, you need your ancestor's full name, the years he served, the service branch, and his company and regiment.

Let's take a tour of the NARA website. Go to *www.archives.gov*, and look for the label *Genealogists* near the left bottom of their home page, and click on that link.

From here, you'll be taken to a page that provides a number of links including *Military Service Records* (on the bottom right-hand side of the screen under *Most Requested* – you may have to scroll down just a bit). Here are the main categories of records NARA has in their collection:

**Bounty Land Warrants**
If you are like me, at one time the only thing I knew about military records (and that was a vague understanding) was about Bounty Land Warrants. The Continental Congress discovered a way to pay its veterans or their widowed and orphaned dependents by giving them public lands. Laws passed between 1776 and 1855 authorized granting warrants for land to those who had served in the Revolutionary War, the War of 1812, the Indian Wars and the Mexican War.

The documents in a Bounty Land Warrant file are similar to those contained in pension files. Veterans needed to prove they had served by providing dates of enlistment and discharge, units in which they served and their commanding officers. If a widow or children of the veteran was applying on behalf of their deceased husband/father, they had to provide marriage and birth dates, the maiden name of the wife, etc. Bounty land warrants can be great finds for genealogical researchers.

Prior to the Revolutionary War, the colonial governments offered military bounty land warrants to men to entice them into military service and they also used them to pay their veterans after the war. These military bounty land warrants began in 1776 and were used until 1855. Until later in the process, the land warrant could only be used in specially designated districts called military districts, primarily Ohio, but also in a few other states, including Arkansas, Georgia, Illinois, Kentucky, Missouri, New York, Pennsylvania, South Carolina, Tennessee, and Virginia. This was a way for the federal government to reward those who served under her flag, and at the same time foster western expansion.

Although the exact number isn't known, researchers of military bounty land warrants have concluded that a very small percentage of veterans actually used their land warrants – perhaps fewer than 10%. Many simply sold their warrants to others

– family, friends, and speculators. The warrant was simply signed, much like endorsing a check, and assigned to someone else. There are no records that indicate who redeemed and who did not redeem their land warrants for themselves, versus selling them to others.

A quick (and short!) note about military bounty land warrants for the Civil War – there were none! In effect from 1776 through 1855, bounty land warrants were used to reward only those veterans who served during the Revolutionary War, War of 1812, some of the Indian Wars and the Mexican-American War.

### Record of Events

Bounty Land Warrants were only good for military service between 1776 and 1855.

Generally, not much of genealogical value is listed in the Records of Events. They are generally sort of journal entries that trace the movement of troops. Often, they are little more than places and dates that the various companies and regiments were stationed or marching to.

These would be of interest if you wanted to trace an ancestor's movements through the war. In the case of the Civil War, it would be interesting to see if any of your ancestors engaged in battles against one another. A number of my ancestors lived in and around border states during the Civil War, and both the Confederate and Union armies had members of my family fighting for them.

### Compiled Military Service Records (CMSR)

Compiled Military Service Records (CMSRs) serve as the records for Union Army soldiers and officers. Each soldier will have one for each regiment in which he served. An index of CMSRs is available on the NARA website. Information found in CMSRs includes biographical and medical information, physical description, pay vouchers, marital status and other personal information like leave requests and commendations. An important distinction about these records: they are only for volunteers who fought in wars. CMSRs were not kept for regular Army soldiers and officers.

**Regular Army Enlistment Papers 1798-1894 and Register of Enlistments in the U.S. Army, 1798–1914**

The federal government did not have CMSRs for the Regular Army. Information about your ancestors who enlisted in the regular army can be found in these enlistment records. Typical enlistment papers show date and place of enlistment, age, place of birth, occupation, physical description, and information about the soldier's company and regiment.

**Regular Army Officers**

CMSRs were not kept for US Army officers, and personnel files were not kept for them until 1863. However, information about officers can be found in a series of letters received by the Adjutant General's office:

• Letters Received by the Office of the Adjutant General, 1805-1821
• Letters Received by the Office of the Adjutant General, 1822-1860
• Letters Received by the Office of the Adjutant General, 1861-1870

This series of letters is available on microfilm through the NARA site. You can either view the microfilm at the NARA main location in Washington DC, or

Another excellent source of information on Army officers is the *Historical Register and Dictionary of the United States Army, From Its Organization, September 29, 1789, to March 2, 1903,* by Francis B. Heitman. This two-volume work provides a snapshot of 100+ years of Army officers. Volume One provides a brief history of each officer, and Volume Two contains a list of battles and actions in

\*Sherman, William Tecumseh. Ohio. Ohio. Cadet M A 1 July 1836 (6); 2 lt 3 art 1 July 1840; 1 lt 30 Nov 1841; capt c s 27 Sept 1850; bvt capt 30 May 1848 for gal and mer ser in Cal dur the war with Mex; resd 6 Sept 1853; col 13 inf 14 May 1861; brig gen vols 17 May 1861; maj gen vols 1 May 1862 to 12 Aug 1864; brig gen U S A 4 July 1863; maj gen 12 Aug 1864; lt gen 25 July 1866; gen 4 Mar 1869; commander-in-chief of the Army 8 Mar 1869 to 1 Nov 1883; retd 8 Feb 1884; by resolution of 19 Feb 1864 the thanks of congs extended—

"To Maj.Gen. W. T. Sherman and the officers and soldiers of the Army of the Tennessee for their gallant and arduous services in marching to the relief of the Army of the Cumberland, and for their gallantry and heroism in the battle of Chattanooga, which contributed in a great degree to the success of our arms in that glorious victory," and by resolution of 10 Jan 1865 "to Maj.Gen. W. T. Sherman and the officers and soldiers of his command for their gallantry and good conduct in their late campaign from Chattanooga to Atlanta, and the triumphal march thence through Georgia to Savannah, terminating in the capture and occupation of that city;" died 14 Feb 1891.

which the US Army engaged. On the previous page is an excerpt for one of the more famous (or infamous, depending on your point of view) generals from the Civil War.

The 1,069-page tome is available to view online at Google Books (just type the title above into the *Search* box of Google). It is fascinating to peruse. Or if you'd like your own copy, you may purchase it at Amazon.com. It was republished in 2010 by Nabu Press. A similar book by T.M.S. Hamersley titled *Army Register of the United States for One Hundred Years, 1779–1879* is also available online. It lists a brief amount of information about each officer from 1779 to 1879. It lists them chronologically, then alphabetically by rank.

### Rendezvous Reports

There are no CMSRs for naval personnel. However, a Rendezvous Report is similar to an enlistment record for the regular Army. *Rendezvous* was the name given to the recruiting station where men could enlist in the navy. The enlistment information was captured and sent to the Navy Department. Rather than enlistment records, they were called "rendezvous reports." They contained similar information as that found in enlistment records: place of residence, date and term of enlistment, occupation and physical description. See below for how to order naval records from NARA.

### Marine Corps Service Records

Some service records were also kept for Marines. These records contain enlistment and reenlistment papers, conduct records, history of their military service, awards and honors and notice of discharge. See below for how to order Marine Corps records from NARA.

### Ordering Navy and Marine Corps Records

Here's what NARA says in the instructions of its form NATF 86 about requesting records for sailors and marines:

### *NAVY OR MARINE CORPS SERVICE RECORDS*

There are no compiled service records for Navy or Marine Corps personnel. Do not use this form to obtain information about obtaining reproductions of records relating to Navy or Marine Corps service. You may obtain information by contacting us online at *www.archives.gov/ contact* or by writing to *Archives 1 Reference (NWCT1F-Military), Textual Archives Services Division, National Archives and Records Administration, 700 Pennsylvania Avenue NW, Washington, DC 20408-0001.*

## Pension Records

Pensions were applied for by military men, their widows and / or their minor children. Because of the need to ensure that the applicant was indeed related to the former soldier, a great deal of information was often requested to substantiate the relationship. A widow, for example, would have had to provide proof that she had been married to the veteran. Documentation could include marriage certificates, property schedules, letters, pages from family Bibles, diaries, journals, or witnesses' affidavits that she had been married to the veteran. She was required to provide the date and place of their marriage (and often the name of the person who performed the marriage). She could often be required to provide either the marriage certificate, or a certified record signed by the minister who performed the ceremony. Sometimes a county clerk could go to the county's marriage register and reproduce the information about the marriage, including the register page, information from that page and an avowal that his was a true reproduction of the information. If the widow had children under the age of 16, she also needed to provide proof of their birth in the form of a birth certificate, or a government-certified document that provided the child's name, birth date and birth place – all genealogical nuggets.

It is important to note that Confederate soldiers' pension applications were made to the state from which they served, not the federal government (I guess the feds decided it was inappropriate to give a federal pension to those who fought to dissolve the union!). Those records are held at the state level.

The vast majority of the records held in the National Archives are paper or on microfilm. They have begun to digitize some of their records, but the process is slow, slow, slow. They have thankfully contracted with for-profit subscription services like Fold3 and Ancestry.com to digitize their records. That's good news for researchers.

From the NARA website, you can search for the various military records that are of interest to you. While all the records can be found at NARA's Washington DC location, some records can also be found at any of NARA's fourteen regional facilities, while others are located at only selected facilities. The NARA website will provide a description of the microfilmed records and will indicate whether they are online through NARA (few are), online through a for-profit subscription service like Fold3 or Ancestry.com, or at one or more of NARA's regional facilities. Following are the locations and websites for NARA's regional facilities:

**Anchorage, Alaska**, e-mail: alaska.archives@nara.gov
Website: www.archives.gov/pacific-alaska/anchorage/index.html

**Laguna Niguel, California**, e-mail: laguna.archives@nara.gov
Website: www.archives.gov/pacific/laguna/index.html

**San Bruno, California**, e-mail: sanbruno.archives@nara.gov
Website: www.archives.gov/pacific/san-francisco/index.html

**Denver, Colorado**, e-mail: denver.archives@nara.gov
Website: www.archives.gov/rocky-mountain/index.html

**East Point, Georgia**, e-mail: atlanta.center@nara.gov
Website: www.archives.gov/southeast/index.html

**Chicago, Illinois**, e-mail: chicago.archives@nara.gov
Website: www.archives.gov/great-lakes/contact/directions-il.html

**Waltham, Massachusetts**, e-mail: waltham.center@nara.gov
Website: www.archives.gov/northeast/boston/

**Pittsfield, Massachusetts**, e-mail: archives@pittsfield.nara.gov
Website: www.archives.gov/northeast/boston/

**Kansas City, Missouri**, e-mail: kansascity.archives@nara.gov
Website: www.archives.gov/facilities/mo/kansas_city.html

**New York, New York**, e-mail: newyork.archives@nara.gov
Website: www.archives.gov/northeast/nyc/

**Philadelphia, Pennsylvania**, e-mail: philadelphia.archives@nara.gov
Website: www.archives.gov/midatlantic/agencies/

**Fort Worth, Texas**, e-mail: ftworth.archives@nara.gov
Website: www.archives.gov/southwest/index.html

**Seattle, Washington**, e-mail: seattle.archives@nara.gov
Website: www.archives.gov/pacific-alaska/seattle/index.html

**Washington DC**, Website: www.archives.gov/

If the records you are searching for are not available online either at NARA or through a subscription service, and you cannot get to a NARA facility, you can order copies of the records. Order forms are available online. Use NATF Form 85, *National Archives Order for Copies of Federal Pension or Bounty Land Warrant Applications*, and Form 86, *National Archives Order for Copies of Military Service Records* to request the specific records you want. Records may be ordered in paper, CD or DVD. Depending on the particular information you are requesting, costs range from $25 to $75 + $.65 per page over 100 pages. The application details the various costs for each request. You will not be charged for a search unless information is located, copied and shipped to you.

Below is the information you will need to request pension, bounty land warrants and service records from NARA. You'll need to complete one of several forms, generally the NATF 85 or NATF 86 form. I've also reproduced for you the NATF

85 form, which you will complete to request pension or bounty land warrant information.

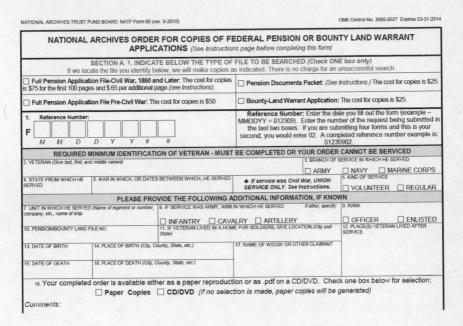

The NATF 86 looks almost the same, except there is no Section A at the top where you identify the type information you are looking for. Both require the veteran's name, state from which he served, war in which he served, and whether he was a volunteer or Regular Army. The NATF 85 requires you to identify the branch of service, while the NATF 86 is only for Regular Army. Both Forms 85 and 86 come with instruction sheets, explaining some of the more vague aspects of the forms as well as providing mailing instructions if you choose to mail your form. You may complete these forms online, or print, complete and mail them.

Note that NARA receives approximately 4,000 requests to pull records daily! That's over 1,000,000 requests each year. No wonder it takes them a little time (typically several weeks at least) to turn around requests.

As mentioned above, many of the records can be viewed in person. (At $25 to $75+ per search, it doesn't take much to justify the cost of a trip, especially if you have multiple lines and ancestors to research!)

*I can order copies of my military ancestor's records from NARA.*

Military records for the 20th century are kept at:

National Personnel Records Center
Military Personnel Records (NPRC-MPR)
9700 Page Avenue
St. Louis, MO 63132-5100

They contain the military personnel, health and medical records of discharged and deceased military veterans from all branches of the armed forces. There are restrictive rules governing the request of a veteran's records by anyone except the veteran. See the instructions for Form 180 that can be found at *www.archives.gov/ research/order/standard-form-180.pdf.*

Records of military personnel prior to 1912 are located in Washington DC at:

National Archives
700 Pennsylvania Avenue
Washington, DC 20408-0001

If you are fortunate enough to go in person to the National Archives, special rules will apply to your visit. For example, you may not bring notebooks, purses or briefcases into the research rooms. Lockers are provided for you to store them in prior to going into the research rooms. You may bring a laptop in as well as a digital camera, although you need permission first to bring the camera in. Notepads will be provided for you, but you must use a pencil, not pens (that keeps unwanted ink from accidentally getting on old documents). As of this writing (but check before you go!), the archives are open to the public from 9:00am to 5:00pm Monday, Tuesday and Saturday, and from 9:00am to 9:00pm Wednesday through Friday.

Special procedures apply when visiting the National Archives.

Note, however, that no pulls (where staff go and pull your requests from the archives) are made from the information stacks on Saturdays. There are four pulls per day Monday and Tuesday, and five per day Wednesday through Friday. The times of these pulls and all these rules will be clarified for you in a short (15- to 20-minute) video you must watch before gaining access to the research rooms.

Now that I've provided you with a general overview of the main records available for your veteran ancestors, we're ready to move on and look at which records apply to which wars.

# 10. WAR-BY-WAR RECORDS

Whether you view records online or visit one of the National Archives locations, you'll want to have an idea of what kinds of records are available for each war. As you would imagine, the earlier the war, the less information will be available. Records for earlier wars are pretty much limited to company and regiment, pay vouchers, muster rolls and if you are lucky, pension applications. Below, war-by-war, are the records available for your perusal.

**Pre-Revolutionary Wars**
Most records of veterans prior to the Revolutionary War will not provide much in the way of genealogical interest. The soldier's name and name of his company and regiment of the colonial units with whom he fought are about the best you can hope for. Few records were kept in those days, and for those that were, many fell prey to fires and carelessness and are no longer available.

But don't despair – the scanty information you find about a military ancestor during this time period may provide clues that lead you to other records. It may give you a clue where they lived at the time of their enlistment. While it is possible that they went to another state to enlist, it is not probable, transportation being what it was in those days. However, you might want to check surrounding states, as, depending on where a fellow lived and where enlistments were taken, it may have been closer for him to ride twenty miles to enlist in neighboring state, than ride one hundred miles to enlist in his own state.

If, for example, you find Ambrose Hawkins listed in a Rhode Island colonial unit during King George's War (1744 to 1748), that may provide a thread for further research, since he had seemingly disappeared from his home state of Massachusetts.

And you might notice that he enlisted in the same unit as a Timothy Hawkins. Brother? Father? Son? Uncle? Cousin? Perhaps he is none of the above, but it is certainly worth noting in your research papers for further research at another time. A few bounty land warrants were issued by the colonial legislatures for service in some of the pre-Revolutionary Wars (French and Indian, King Philip's War, etc.).

**Revolutionary War**

To see what records may be available for your Revolutionary War ancestor, go to *www.archives.gov/research/military/american-revolution/*, then click on the hyperlink *Search Documents Online* in the middle of the page.

The page you'll be directed to describes what records are available, and what formats. Although few, there are some Revolutionary War documents online. You can see their online collection by clicking on the link that says: *Search documents online*. Near the top left-hand corner of the page is a yellow *Search* button – click that, then enter *Revolutionary War* in the *Search* box. I changed the maximum number of hits to be displayed to 1000 (the default is 100), and then typed *Revolutionary War*, and received 870 hits.

Descriptions of available collections will greet you, all of them with links that will take you to other pages that will provide more information on the collections – a description of the collection, format(s) available, etc. For example, as of this writing, the first link that comes up is:

**Numbered Record Books**
*compiled 1894 - 1913, documenting the period 1775 - 1798*
Clicking on the link takes me to a page that provides further information. The first tab is labeled *Details*, and provides information about the collection: type of record, range of years covered, and how to order copies of the collection. And – you want to look for this: it will also tell you whether or not the record has been digitized, and if so, by whom, and provides a link to that source. That's an exciting find! Typically the digitizing resource will be Fold3 or Ancestry.com, depending on the collection.

The second tab for this collection is *Scope & Content*, and clicking on that provides me a description of the collection:

> This series documents Revolutionary War activities and consists of orderly books, rosters of soldiers, oaths of allegiance, commissions of officers, receipts, accounts, copies of letters sent, and other records relating to the Departments of the Quartermaster General and the Commissary General of Military Stores, along with records relating to pay and the settlement of accounts.

The third tab labeled *Archived Copies* tells me where the records are kept and what format they are in (paper, microfilm, microfiche, bound volume, etc.).

I can narrow my search by providing more qualifiers on my *Search* query: for example, *Revolutionary War Pensions*. When I did that, I got 281 hits, the first of which was:

**Case Files of Pension and Bounty-Land Warrant Applications Based on Revolutionary War Service**
*compiled ca. 1800 - ca. 1912, documenting the period ca. 1775 - ca. 1900*
When you review the information about these records, what you hope to see is another tab next to the *Archived Copies* tab that says, *Digital Copies*. That means NARA has digitized this set of records and they are available for you to view online. Most will not be digitized, especially the earlier records. However, as mentioned above, some have been digitized by subscription services. The *Detail* tab for this collection has this entry:

> **Online Resource:** Fold3
> **Online Resource URL:** *www.Fold3/documents/10936943/revolutionary-war-pensions*
> **Online Resource Notes:** Records in this series have been digitized and made available online by our partner, Fold3, for a fee. The digitized records on Fold3 are available free of charge in all NARA Research Rooms, including those in our regional archives and Presidential Libraries.

Fold3 and Ancestry.com are digitizing many of the NARA military records.

So as you can see, this collection hasn't been digitized by NARA, but it has been digitized by Fold3. A great find! Now, I happen to have a subscription to Fold3 (good deal), so I whisked to their website to see what I could find. As a stab in the dark, I typed in *Revolutionary War Quillen*, and received sixty hits. I selected Robert Quillen, and found the following:

Robert Quillen
1st Virginia Regiment
Private

There wasn't any information on the card beyond his name, rank and regiment, but at the end of the card, there was a comment that said his records were filed under the name Robert *Quillin* – apparently the difficulties of getting my surname correct extend back to at least that time! I checked there, and there were a number of records for Robert *Quillin*, including a payroll record (which indicated he was paid $6.67 per month for his service!), his compiled service record, and numerous muster sheets (roll calls). I also found that he received a bounty land warrant for his service, issued February 1808 (nothing like timely payment for his service – three decades after the fact!).

I decided to see if Fold3 had a pension application for Robert – remember, pension applications often contain significant amounts of genealogical data. I typed in *Revolutionary War Pensions Quillin*, and….alas, no such luck – either Robert didn't file an application, or he did and it hasn't yet been digitized (or perhaps he filed an application and it has been lost to history). But – even though Robert's application wasn't there, there were 17 hits on my request. Among them I found the pension application for John Quillin. Below are excerpts from his pension application – I have **highlighted in bold** the **genealogical data** that exist in the document:

> **State of North Carolina**
> **Stokes County**
> On this **24th day of August, 1833**, personally appeared unto me…John

Quillin, **aged seventy-six years,** who being first sworn according to law **at his own place of residence** in the afore-mentioned county, doth on his Oath make the following declaration in order to obtain the benefit of the Act of Congress passed 7th June 1832. First he states that from the infirmities of old age together with the fact that at certain times the loss of his memory makes it impossible for him to remember the precise dates of his service as a soldier of the Revolution, but as well as he can recollect, he entered the service of the United States under the following named officers who served as hereinafter stated. That he first entered the service as a drafted private in Surry County, North Carolina in Captain Henry Smith's company of militia infantry….(following this were officers' names and descriptions of campaigns John was on)….Near the Savannah River, the applicant states that he hired a certain William Fields as a substitute to serve the balance of his tour in order that he might **return home to his wife who was in a delicate situation** at the time…

Of the seven interrogatories prescribed by the War Department, he answers them as follows (to wit):

1st – that **he was born in Cumberland County, North Carolina**

2nd – that he has no record of his age, only traditionary that **he was born in March 1757**

3rd – that he lived **in Surry County North Carolina when called into the service….**

4th – answer as above

5th – that from his being subject to fitts and consequent loss of his recollection, he cannot name all the officers any more than he has named already or Regiments

6th – that he does not remember of receiving a written discharge, and if he did, he has lost it

7th – he has no one present, but has a number of individuals that will testify as to his character as to veracity and belief of his services as a soldier of the Revolution, there being no clergyman for a considerable distance from him renders it very inconvenient for one's certificate.

The pension application was signed by the attorney and Justice of the Peace (same man) who took his testimony and statement. There were ten pages in the pension application, including the cover of the envelope all the papers were in, as well as seven other pages, including statements from several neighbors and a man who averred that he served with John during parts of his service. But let's check out the genealogical information available from this pension application:

1. **State of North Carolina, Stokes County** – identifies where John was on a certain date;
2. **24 August, 1833** – the certain date John was at Stokes County, NC;
3. **...at his own place of residence...** — The statement was taken at his residence on the above date in the above-stated county and state;
4. **aged seventy-six** — he was seventy-six (76) years old on 24 August 1833;
5. **return home to his wife** — He was married;
6. **his wife who was in a delicate situation** – this was often a euphemism for pregnancy (but could also have meant she was very ill);
7. **born in Cumberland County, North Carolina** – John's birth place;
8. **he was born in March 1757** – John's birth month and date, according to *traditionary....*

As you can see, this 250-year-old document has a cache of wonderful genealogical tidbits for us for this gentleman, a patriotic if not failing-memoried soldier of the Revolution!

(**Author's note:** I selected John Quillin's pension more or less out of a hat to demonstrate this research source and technique. Some of the information – like his first name and place of birth — seemed familiar, and I turned to some of my genealogy records to see how closely we were related. I discovered that my fifth great grandfather was John Quillin, born March 1757 in Cumberland County, North Carolina – this very man! Another genealogical coincidence!)

Pension applications contain a TON of genealogical information!

Back to the NARA website, following are a few of the 100s of Revolutionary War records that are available:

- Revolutionary War Rolls, 1775 – 1783
- Compiled Service Records, 1775 – 1784
- Indexes to Compiled Service Records, 1775 – 1783
- Case Files of Pension and Bounty-Land Warrant Applications Based on Revolutionary War Service, ca. 1775 - ca. 1900
- Lists of Revolutionary War Officers, 1775 — 1783
- Bounty Land Application Warrant Application Files, 1812 – 1855
- Registers of Muster Rolls, 1775 – 1782
- **Benedict Arnold's Oath of Allegiance** (okay – so unless you are related to Benedict Arnold, there isn't much genealogical value here, but I just thought it was interesting!)

And over 800 more collections!

You'll note one of the last links I listed had to do with bounty land warrants. We discussed those gems in the previous chapter. For the Revolutionary War, the Continental Congress provided bounty land warrants in several denominations: privates and non-commissioned officers qualified for 100 acres, captains for 300 acres up to 1,100 acres for generals. In addition, nine of the original colonies / states offered bounty land warrants to soldiers who served from their states. Those awards varied from 50 to 640 acres for privates. Generals fared much better…state bounty land warrants ranged between 0 acres (Georgia and New York) and 25,000 acres (North Carolina).

Many of the Revolutionary War bounty land warrants are included in the pension files of veterans of that war. Fold3 has a collection with over 2.3 million records of veterans in it.

As you examine the various Revolutionary War links on the NARA website, you'll note that numerous of the links you select warn you that most of the records from the Revolutionary War period were destroyed by fire in 1800 or in 1814, the latter due to the hostilities surrounding the War of 1812. According to the NARA website, the current collection housed in the National Archives was:

...begun in 1873 by means of purchase, gifts, or transfers from other agencies. The compilation of military service records was begun in 1894, under the direction of the War Department's Record and Pension Office. Information about individual soldiers was meticulously copied onto cards as a means of consolidating information about individuals, as well as preserving the original source documents, including muster rolls, pay rolls, returns, and other records.

## War of 1812

Just to brush you up on your history. The war of 1812 was fought on US soil and in US coastal waters from 1812 to 1815, between the United States and its former parent and nemesis, Great Britain. It was the War of 1812 that gave us the National Anthem (you thought it was the Revolutionary War, didn't you?!).

Now that you have had your tour of the NARA website from the previous section, you should be able to use the same directions to find records from the War of 1812. At the time of this writing, it was difficult to find the *Search* box for the War of 1812, similar to the one available for the Revolutionary War, so here is a shortcut to that website: *http://arcweb.archives.gov/arc/action/BasicSearchForm*. Heading there, when I enter *War of 1812*, I get over 850 record collections related to the War of 1812.

In addition to NARA's collection, Ancestry.com has compiled the information for nearly 600,000 men who served during the War of 1812, and those records are online. While you won't be able to see an image of the original document, they have summarized (compiled) the information from each service record. At a minimum, you'll be able to see if an ancestor was enlisted during the War of 1812, his state, company / regiment and rank. This is all important information – remember NATF Forms 85 and 86, which are required to order most military records, require your ancestor's name, state from which he served and company / regiment.

The NARA website contains an excellent article entitled *Genealogical Records of the War of 1812*, written by Stuart L. Butler (currently located at *www.archives.gov/publications/prologue/1991/winter/war-of-1812.html*). If you are looking for ancestors from this time period, it would be worth your time to read what he has written. Searching the NARA website yields, among others, the following War of 1812 collections that might be worth reviewing:

• War of 1812 Prize Case files, 1812 – 1816
• Pension and Bounty Land Warrant Application Files, 1812 – 1900.
• Carded Records Showing Military Service of Soldiers Who Fought in Volunteer Organizations During the War of 1812, 1812 – 1815.
• Index to War of 1812 Pension Application Files, 1812 – 1816
• Muster of Volunteers organized during War of 1812, 1812 – 1815.

And over 500 additional collections!

Bounty land warrants deserve a brief mention here. Veterans of the War of 1812 qualified for a bounty land warrant if they enlisted in regiments raised by Congress and if they served for five years or more. Congress created three special military districts where these bounty land warrants were good: Arkansas, Illinois and Missouri.

If you Google *War of 1812 war records*, you'll be surprised at how many sites come up devoted to this war, especially many outside of the NARA holdings. Here are a few:

• *indiamond6.ulib.iupui.edu/War1812/* — a listing of Indiana residents who were veterans of the War of 1812;
• *www.sos.mo.gov/archives/soldiers/* — database containing information about Missouri residents who were veterans of the War of 1812;
• *www.portal.state.pa.us/portal/server.pt/community/military_records/3186/ war_of_1812/388404* — a roster of all Pennsylvania residents who served in the War of 1812;
• *www.ohiohistory.org/museums-and-historic-sites/museum—historic-sites-by-topic/ military* — the Ohio Historical Society index to the roster of Ohio War of 1812 veterans.

And so on – many states kept documentation on the War of 1812, and many of their records are available online.

In addition, Ancestry.com and Fold3 have a number of collections from the War of 1812, but still pretty limited, all things considered. However, both services had made significant progress in the collections they had digitized since the last time I checked for this war. As an example, when I checked Ancestry.com's collection about six months prior to this writing, they had just a handful of collections, but this time when I checked they had a number more, including one titled *War of 1812 Pension File Index*. I knew it would only be an *index* of those who had filed pension applications (not the actual pension application), but I thought I would check and see if my fourth great grandfather, Samuel Horney, had filed a pension application, since he was a veteran of both the War of 1812 and the Mexican War. The index is actually a digital image of the outside of the pension envelope for each veteran, arranged alphabetically. The compiler had the opportunity to complete the following information about the veteran on the outside of the envelope:

- Veteran's name
- Veteran's rank, unit and commanding officer
- Pension application number
- Bounty Land Warrant number
- Widow's name
- Enlistment and discharge dates
- Residence of veteran
- Residence of widow
- Maiden name of widow
- Marriage date of veteran
- Death date of veteran
- Death date of widow
- A section for remarks

I found Samuel's name in the index, along with several pension file numbers, his rank, state from which he served, military unit and commanding officer. Until the War of 1812 files go online, either by NARA, Fold3, Ancestry.com or someone else, my only option now is to order the pension file from NARA. But it is an option, and now I have two pension file numbers to reference, telling me that he did file applications, and also boosting the chances that the actual file will be found.

If you are fortunate, the individual compiling the pension file for your ancestor took the time to complete other than the basics of the pension file. While my fourth great grandfather's file didn't have the additional information shown above, about 25% of the records I looked at provided most of that information on the envelope. There were several periods where veterans of the War of 1812 could apply for pensions. The first only granted pensions in the case of the death or disability due to wounds of the veteran. But there were two additional Acts of Congress that allowed pensions based on service alone. In 1871 an Act was passed allowing pensions for War of 1812 veterans or their widows if they had served at least 60 days, and if it was a widow making application, the couple had to be married prior to 17 February 1815 – the date the peace treaty was ratified. The next Act was passed in 1878 and provided a pension to those who had served for at least 14 days or who had been in any battle. This Act had no requirement as to the date of marriage of the couple.

> Bounty Land Warrants were issued to veterans of the War of 1812 and the Mexican War.

## Mexican-American War

The Mexican War was fought between 1846 and 1848. It was a training ground for many of the soldiers and officers who would later fight side-by-side or nose-to-nose (as foes) in the American Civil War.

Here is a shortcut to that website where you can discover NARA's holdings for this war: *http://arcweb.archives.gov/arc/action/BasicSearchForm*. Heading there, when I enter *Mexican-American War* I get nearly 600 record collections related to that conflict.

Enlistment, muster records and pension applications are available for veterans of the Mexican-American War, as are bounty land warranty applications. Bounty land warrant applications are included with the pension applications for the Mexican-American War. These records are available through NARA:

• Carded Records Showing Military Service of Soldiers Who Fought in Volunteer
  Organizations During the Mexican War, compiled 1899 - 1927, documenting the period 1846 - 1848

• Case Files of Mexican War Pension Applications, compiled ca. 1887 - ca. 1926, documenting the period ca. 1846 - ca. 1926

• Returns of Army Commands in the War of 1812, Mexican War and Civil War, compiled 1812 - 1865

• Name Index to Pension Applications Files of Remarried Widows Based on Service Before 1861, compiled 1887 - 1926

• Registers of Applications for Bounty Land Warrants, compiled 04/1855 - 08/1863

• Ancestry.com and Fold3 have a number of collections from the Mexican-American War; their collections are still pretty limited, but growing all the time.

**Civil War**

Over 2.8 million American men (and a few hundred women) served during the Civil War – about 7% of the population. And when you figure that roughly 50% the of population were men, that means that approximately 14% of the males in the United States served during the Civil War – about 1 in 7. So if your ancestor was between the ages of 18 and 45 during the Civil War years, there's a good chance you'll find information about him in military records of one of the respective armies.

There are many records available for veterans of the Civil War. Unfortunately, many of these records are still not digitized, and are only available through a personal visit to the National Archives, or through ordering copies.

**Civil War Soldiers and Sailors System (CWSS)**

There are a number of ways to learn whether your ancestor fought in the Civil War. One of the best is the Civil War Soldiers and Sailors System (CWSS). It will tell you whether an ancestor served, what branch of the service he was in and even whether he served with the Union or the Confederacy. To start your search, go to *www.civilwar.nps.gov/cwss*, and then select *Soldiers* or *Sailors*, then enter the name of your ancestor. Many generations of my Quillen ancestors lived in the southwestern tip of Virginia, near the confluence of Tennessee, North Carolina, Kentucky and Virginia. The vast majority of her sons served the Confederacy. At the same time, the Cunningham branch of my family was from central Pennsylvania, and the vast majority of that state served in the Union army. Here are a couple of records I found:

| Soldier's name: | Charles C. Quillen | Hugh Cunningham |
|---|---|---|
| Regiment name: | 37th Virginia Infantry | 63rd Pennsylvania Infantry |
| Side: | Confederate | Union |
| Soldier's Rank – In: | Private | Private |
| Soldier's Rank – Out: | Corporal | Corporal |
| Alternate name: | Charles C. Quillin | H. Cunningham |
| Notes: | | |
| Film Number: | M382, roll 45 | M554, roll 25 |

Both of these men are distant relatives of mine. And the infantry units for which these men fought were involved in many battles, including Gettysburg. Sigh…

Most of the information from this website is easily understandable. The film number is the NARA microfilm number where this information was found.

Back on the CWSS title page, you can click on the *Regiment* link to find a history of your ancestor's regiment – its formation date and place, major battles and assignments it received, total lost officers and soldiers, etc.

The CWSS title page also provides links to Congressional Medal of Honor Winners, prisoner records for Union prisoners held at Andersonville and Confederate prisoners held at Fort McHenry, and the location of graves for soldiers buried at National Parks (like Gettysburg). There is also a link to information about over 10,500 battles and skirmishes fought during the Civil War. Of those encounters, 384 were considered principal battles.

While all of these tidbits of information are interesting, they provide an important piece of information: your ancestor's army (Union or Confederate), the state from which he served, and his regiment number. Using this information, you can order copies of your ancestor's service records from NARA.

> The CWSS website provides important information about my Civil War ancestor soldiers.

Many of the soldiers who were involved in the Civil War fought with state militias. Military records for those units are held at the state level. If that's the case, you are in luck, as many of the state records have been digitized and are available online. If the state militia became part of the regular army, their records will also be held at the National Archives.

Following are records that should be searched for your Civil War veteran ancestors:

**Union Army Records**
There are far more records available for soldiers who served in the Union army than there are for those who served in the Confederate army. For those ancestors who served in the Union Army, there are four groups of records that are of particular interest:

• Draft records
• Compiled Military Service Records (CMSR)
• Pension applications
• Compiled Records showing service of military units in volunteer Union organizations

**Draft Records**
In March 1863, the federal government instituted a draft for all men ages 20 to 45. The draft ran through the end of the war in 1865. The information listed in the draft records included:

• Name
• Place of residence
• Place of birth (sometimes)
• Age as of July 1, 1863
• Occupation
• Marital status
• State, territory or country of birth (naturalized citizens were eligible for the draft, as were those who had stated their intention to naturalize)

105

• Military organization (if he was already in a volunteer unit)
• Physical description (sometimes)

Men in this age range were exempt from service if:

• They were in the military of the United States at the time of the draft
• They served in the US military during the present war, and were honorably discharged
• They were physically or mentally disabled
• They paid someone to take their place ($300 to $1,000)
• They were the only son of a widow
• They were the sole support for infirm parents
• They were a widower with dependents

The government did not keep records of those who were exempted; rather lists of those who were exempted may be found in local newspapers of the time. They are often grouped by their exemption class.

As interesting and information-filled as they are, none of the draft records have been microfilmed. They are kept by state and congressional district within each state. Congressional districts from the Civil War era can be found in *The Historical Atlas of United States Congressional Districts 1789 – 1983* (Kenneth C. Martis, New York: The Free Press). Most larger libraries – especially those with genealogy sections – will have this book available. Also, some diligent searching on the internet should be able to locate congressional districts from 1860 in each state. At the time of this writing, your only option for seeing draft records is to either visit the National Archives in Washington DC or mail a request for a copy of the draft record using NATF form 86 for your request. You may also order online by going to *eservices.archives.gov/orderonline*.

**Compiled Military Service Records**
As a reminder, every volunteer soldier had a Compiled Military Service Record (CMSR) for each regiment he served in. It contains basic information about his service while in that regiment. Information contained within the record might include enlistment information, leave (vacation) requests, muster (roll call) records,

and injury or illness reports. If your ancestor was killed in action, this will most likely be found in the CMSR, or information about his discharge if he survived. An index of CMSRs is available on the NARA website as well as on the CWSS website. When I requested the service record for Colonel Leonidas Horney, my third great grandfather, I received documents that included the following:

- The date and place of his enlistment;
- His date of birth;
- His height, hair and eye color and color of complexion;
- The rank he enlisted as;
- The name of his regiment and company;
- The commanders he reported to;
- Several muster sheets showing his presence on specific dates (muster sheets are like roll calls);
- A copy of a letter from his commanding officer granting him a two-month leave;
- Several documents detailing his promotion from Captain to Major to Lieutenant Colonel;
- Two casualty sheets, one detailing a slight leg injury sustained at the Battle of Corinth and the other reporting his death in the Battle of Champion Hill, Mississippi on May 16, 1863.

## Pension Records

As mentioned at the outset of this chapter, pension records often provide us with a great deal of information. When I searched for the Civil War pension record for Colonel Horney, I found a great deal of information about him and his family. As shown at the outset of this chapter, after Leonidas's death, his widow completed a series of affidavits that contained the following information:

- Her full maiden name;
- Her age and birth date;
- Her birth place;
- The date and place she married her husband;
- The name of the person who performed their marriage ceremony;
- The names, birth dates and ages of all their children 16 years of age and younger;

• The names and birth dates of those children who had died.

That was truly a great genealogical find!

Copies of pension records for Union army soldiers can be gotten by sending NATF Form 85 (not Form 86; Form 85 is used for pensions). You may also order online by going to *eservices.archives.gov/orderonline*.

## Confederate Army Records

There are fewer records available for the Confederate Army, as many did not survive the war; those that are available are:

• Compiled Military Service Records
  • Compiled Records showing service of military units in volunteer Confederate organizations

Note: The federal government did not grant pensions to Confederate soldiers (imagine that!); but all states that had Confederate soldiers later granted pensions.

## Compiled Military Service Records (CMSR)

As with the Union army, every Confederate soldier had a Compiled Military Service Record (CMSR) for each regiment he served in.

Both CMSRs and Records of Events were kept for Confederate units. They are often not as complete as Union records of the same type, as many Confederate records did not survive the war. Pensions were granted to Confederate veterans and their widows and minor children by the states of Alabama, Arkansas, Florida, Georgia, Kentucky, Louisiana, Mississippi, Missouri, North Carolina, Oklahoma, South Carolina, Tennessee, Texas, and Virginia. Since the *states* granted these pensions, not the federal government; those records are contained in the State Archives of the state where the veteran resided after the war, not in the National Archives.

Copies of Confederate army records held in the National Archives can be ordered by sending NATF Form 86. You may also order online by going to *eservices.archives.gov/orderonline*.

## Pension Records

As mentioned above, pension records can be a valuable source of genealogical information. Each state decided at different times when and if they would provide pensions to Confederate veterans, and who was eligible for those pensions. Below is the contact information of the offices for each of the states that granted Confederate pensions, and a little about their collections:

Confederate pension records are held at the state level.

**Alabama Department of Archives and History**
Telephone: 334/242-4363
Website: *www.archives.state.al.us/index.html*

In 1867 Alabama began granting pensions to Confederate veterans who had lost arms or legs. In 1886 the State began granting pensions to veterans' widows. In 1891 the law was amended to grant pensions to indigent veterans or their widows.

**Arkansas History Commission**
Telephone: 501/682-6900
Website: *www.ark-ives.com*

In 1891 Arkansas began granting pensions to indigent Confederate veterans. In 1915 the State began granting pensions to their widows and mothers.

**Florida State Archives**
Telephone: 850/487-2073
Website: *www.dlis.dos.state.fl.us/index_researchers.cfm*

In 1885 Florida began granting pensions to Confederate veterans. In 1889 the State began granting pensions to their widows. A published index, which provides each veteran's pension number, is available in many libraries.

**Georgia Department of Archives and History**
Telephone: 678/364-3700
Website: *www.sos.state.ga.us/archives/*

In 1870 Georgia began granting pensions to soldiers with artificial limbs. In 1879 the State began granting pensions to other disabled Confederate veterans or their widows who then resided in Georgia. By 1894 eligible disabilities had been expanded to include old age and poverty.

**Kentucky Department of Libraries and Archives**
Telephone: 502/564-8704
Website: *kdla.ky.gov/Pages/default.aspx*

In 1912, Kentucky began granting pensions to Confederate veterans or their widows. The records are on microfilm.

**Louisiana State Archives**
Telephone: 504/922-1208
Website: *www.sos.louisiana.gov/tabid/53/Default.aspx*

In 1898 Louisiana began granting pensions to indigent Confederate veterans or their widows.

**Mississippi Department of Archives and History**
Telephone: 601/359-6876
Website*: www.mdah.state.ms.us/*

In 1888 Mississippi began granting pensions to indigent Confederate veterans or their widows.

**Missouri State Archives**
Telephone: 573/751-3280
Website: *www.sos.mo.gov/archives/*

In 1911 Missouri began granting pensions to indigent Confederate veterans only; none were granted to widows. Missouri also had a home for disabled Confederate veterans. The pension and veterans' home applications are interfiled and arranged alphabetically.

**North Carolina State Archives**

Telephone: 919/733-7305

Website: *www.ah.dcr.state.nc.us/archives/*

In 1867 North Carolina began granting pensions to Confederate veterans who were blinded or lost an arm or leg during their service. In 1885 the State began granting pensions to all other disabled indigent Confederate veterans or widows.

**Oklahoma Department of Libraries, Archives and Records Management Division**

Telephone: 800/522-8116 (nationwide) ext. 209

Website: *www.odl.state.ok.us*

In 1915 Oklahoma began granting pensions to Confederate veterans or their widows.

**South Carolina Department of Archives and History**

Telephone: 803/896-6100

Website: *www.state.sc.us/scdah*

A state law enacted December 24, 1887, permitted financially needy Confederate veterans and widows to apply for a pension; however, few applications survive from the 1888-1918 era. From 1919 to 1925, South Carolina granted pensions to Confederate veterans and widows regardless of financial need. Also available are Confederate Home applications and inmate records for veterans (1909-1957), and applications of wives, widows, sisters, and daughters (1925-1955).

**Tennessee State Library and Archives**

Telephone: 615/741-2764

Website: *www.tennessee.gov/tsla/*

In 1891 Tennessee began granting pensions to indigent Confederate veterans. In 1905 the State began granting pensions to their widows. The records are on microfilm.

**Texas State Library and Archives Commission**
Telephone: 512/463-5480
Website: *www.tsl.state.tx.us/arc/genfirst.html (Genealogy)*
Website: *www.tsl.state.tx.us/arc/index.html* (Archives and Manuscripts)

In 1881 Texas set aside 1,280 acres for disabled Confederate veterans. In 1889 the State began granting pensions to indigent Confederate veterans and their widows. Muster rolls of State militia in Confederate service are also available.

**Library of Virginia**
Telephone: 804/692-3888
Website: *www.lva.lib.va.us/*

In 1888 Virginia began granting pensions to Confederate veterans or their widows. The records are on microfilm.

In addition to these records, the Family History Library of the Church of Jesus Christ of Latter-day Saints has a large collection of microfilmed Confederate records. They can be seen in Salt Lake City, or ordered for viewing at any local family history center. You can start learning about their collection by going to *www.familysearch.org,* click on *Search,* then Wiki, after which you will enter *Confederate* in the *Search* box.

If you are a genealogist researching ancestors who were between the ages of 20 and 50 in the 1860s, it's a pretty sure bet that at least some of them served in the Civil War. If that's the case, you may well find a great deal of genealogical information for them through Civil War records. Of all the wars America has had, the Civil War is the most laden with genealogical gems. Because of the intense interest in this war – both on the part of genealogists as well as historians, many of these records are becoming available online at a rapid pace.

In addition to the records I have listed here, any source you go to that has Civil War collections will have a seemingly endless list of records from this war. Prisoner's records, state censuses of their sons who fought and died, Union soldier tombstones, Confederate soldier tombstones, Confederate state field officers and so on.

Many are of limited genealogical value, but may provide slivers of clues for you if you are running into brick walls on any given soldier.

When searching for Civil War records, don't forget your old friend Google. So many genealogy societies are putting Civil War records online on almost a daily basis. I have had great success using Google to find many military records, Civil War and earlier.

And remember – when you go to look for bounty land warrants for Civil War veterans – don't. None were issued as a result of the Civil War.

## World War I

When the hostilities broke out that thrust America into World War I, Congress passed the Selective Service Act, which required all men between the ages of 21 and 31 as of June 5, 1917 to register. A year later, another registration was required for those who had turned 21 since the previous draft. A third (also called supplemental) draft registration required all men who would turn 21 by August 24, 1918 to register. Finally, on September 12, 1918, all men between the ages of 18 and 45 (born between September 11, 1872 and September 12, 1900) were required to register for the draft. One of the richest genealogical finds from World War I are the draft registration cards for the 24,000,000 men living in the United States who registered for the draft — approximately 98% of the men living in America at the time, so it is highly probable that if your male ancestor was between 21 and 45 years of age during that time, he completed a World War I draft registration card.

As mentioned above, there were three different draft registration periods covering three different classes of men. Of course, it would have been too easy to use the same registration card for each period (but they didn't!). Generally, the information requested the following information for these men:

> Of the men ages 18 to 45, 98% registered for the draft during World War I.

- Full name
- Home address
- Age in years
- Birth date

- Race
- Native born, naturalized or alien
- If an alien, what country are they a citizen of
- Occupation
- Employer's name
- Employer's place of business
- Nearest relative
- Nearest relative's address
- Brief physical description (height, weight, build, hair and eye color)
- Signature of the registrant

From a genealogical perspective, what's not to love about such a record?!

There is another benefit to these records. Many states did not require birth records to be kept until either the late 19th or early 20th century. As these 24,000,000 men completed their draft registration cards, they may have been creating the only government document that had their birth information on it. It is considered a secondary source, but still an important source of information.

Through the years we have pondered about and researched what my great grandfather's birthday and birth place were. Depending on which census we looked at, his birthday was reported as January 1880, January 1881 and October 1881. His birth place had been reported as Virginia and Tennessee. Of course, we didn't know if he was providing that information or if someone else in the household had been providing the information, and was remembering incorrectly. But his World War I draft registration card tells us what *he* believed:

- Name – Ed Quillen
- Home address – RR 1, Ralston, Pawnee County, Oklahoma
- Age in years — 37
- Birth date – January 15, 1881
- Race — White
- Native born
- Occupation — Farmer

- Employer's name
- Employer's place of business
- Nearest relative – Wife — Dollie Quillen
- Nearest relative's address – RR 1, Ralston, Pawnee Co., Oklahoma
- Brief physical description: 5'11", medium build, black hair, blue eyes

Since each draft registration period used a slightly different draft registration card, I have provided a facsimile of the card used for each registration on pages 115-120. You may either print each card and use it as a template for writing down the information you find for your ancestors, or you can simply use it to decipher the questions that were asked – some of the microfilmed documents are difficult to read. The following pages contain those templates.

Note – If you would like to get these online, you can also download them from our website at *www.essentialgenealogy.com/forms__records.*
.

Every male between the ages identified by each draft was required to complete a draft registration card if he was living in America at this time. That included aliens, whether they had been naturalized or not. What that means for you is that any male ancestors you have who were born between September 11, 1872 and September 12, 1900 will most likely (98% chance) have completed one of these draft registration cards. This may allow you to find more about his place of birth, or confirm information you already know. In my *Mastering Immigration and Naturalization* book, I share an example of doing just that.

You can find these World War I draft registration cards at some of the following locations:

1. The National Archives
2. Ancestry.com
3. Other pay-for-service genealogy services
4. Family History Library of the LDS Church
5. Other free locations

**Draft Registration Card used during the June 5, 1917 Registration – Page 1**
**For all men between the ages of 21 and 31**

| | REGISTRATION CARD | |
|---|---|---|
| 1 | Name in full _____ <br> (Given name)　　　　(Family name) | Age in Years |
| 2 | Home <br> _____ <br> Address　　(No)　　(Street)　　(City)　　(State) | |
| 3 | Date of Birth <br> _____ <br> 　　　(Month)　　　(Day)　　　(Year) | |
| 4 | Are you (1) a natural-born citizen, (2) a naturalized citizen, (3) an alien, (4) or have you declared your intention (specify which)? <br> _____ | |
| 5 | Where were you born? <br> _____ <br> 　　　　(Town)　　　(State)　　　(Nation) | |
| 6 | If not a citizen, of what nation are you a citizen or subject? <br> _____ | |
| 7 | What is your present trade, occupation, or office? <br> _____ | |
| 8 | By whom employed? _____ <br><br> Where employed? _____ | |
| 9 | Have you a father, mother, wife, child under 12, or a sister or brother under 12, solely dependent on you for support (specify which)? <br> _____ | |
| 10 | Married or single (which)? <br> _____ | |
| 11 | What military service have you had? <br> Rank _____Branch_____ <br> Years _____ Nation or state _____ | |
| 12 | Do you claim exemption <br> From draft (specify grounds)? _____ | |
| | I affirm that I have verified above answers and that they are true <br> _____ <br> (Signature or mark) <br> If person is of African descent, <br> cut off this corner | |

**Draft Registration Card used during the June 5, 1917 Registration – Page 2**

| | **REGISTRAR'S REPORT** |
|---|---|
| 1 | Tall, medium, or short (specify which)? _____ <br> Slender, medium, or stout (which)? _____ |
| 2 | Color of eyes _____Color of hair _____ Bald _____ |
| 3 | Has person lost arm, leg, hand, foot, eye, or both eyes or is he otherwise disabled (specify)? _____ |

I certify that my answers are true, that the person registered has read his own answers, that I have witnessed his signature, and that all of his answers of which I have knowledge are true, except as follows:

_____

_____

_____

_____

(Signature of Registrar)

Precinct _____

City or County _____    _____

State _____    (Date of Registration)

**Draft Registration Card used during the June 5, 1918 Registration – Page 1**
**For all men becoming 21 after June 5, 1918**

| | | |
|---|---|---|
| Serial No. _____ | | Registration No. _____ |

| 1 | Name in full _____ <br>           (Given name)          (Family name) | Age in Years |
|---|---|---|
| 2 | Home Address <br> _____ <br>    (No)    (Street or RFD)   (City or Town)     (State) | |
| 3 | Date of Birth _____ <br>              (Month)        (Day)      (Year) | |
| 4 | Where were you born? <br> _____ <br>     (City or Town)      (State)      (Nation) | |
| 5 |     1. Native of the United States <br>     2. Naturalized Citizen <br>     3. Alien <br>     4. Declared Intention <br>     5. Noncitizen or citizen Indian <br> (Strike our items or words not applicable) | |
| 6 | If not a citizen, of what nation are you a citizen or subject? _____ | |
| 7 | Father's Birth place <br> _____ <br>     (City or Town)      (State)     (Nation) | |
| 8 | Name of employer <br> _____ <br><br> Place of employment <br> _____ <br>    (No)    (Street or RFD)   (City or Town)     (State) | |
| 9 | Name of nearest relative <br> _____ <br> Address of nearest relative <br> _____ <br>    (No)    (Street or RFD)   (City or Town)     (State) | |
| 10 | Race – White, Negro, Indian <br>     (Strike our items or words not applicable) | |

I affirm that I have verified above answers and that they are true

                   P.M.G.O          _____
                   Form 1          (Signature or mark)

If person is of
African descent,
cut off this corner         REGISTRATION CARD

**Draft Registration Card used during the June 5, 1918 Registration – Page 2**

<table>
<tr><td colspan="2" align="center">REGISTRAR'S REPORT</td></tr>
<tr><td>1</td><td>Tall<br>Medium<br>Short         (Strike out words not applicable)<br><br>Slender<br>Medium<br>Stout</td></tr>
<tr><td>2</td><td>Color of eyes _____    Color of hair _____</td></tr>
<tr><td>3</td><td>Has person lost arm, leg, hand, foot, eye, or is he<br>palpably physically disqualified (specify)?<br>_____<br>_____<br>_____</td></tr>
</table>

I certify that my answers are true, that the person registered has read his own answers, that I have witnessed his signature, and that all of his answers of which I have knowledge are true, except as follows:

_____

_____

_____

_____

_____

(Signature of Registrar)

_____

Date of Registration)

(The stamp of the local board having jurisdiction of the area in which the registrant has his appointment shall be placed in this box)

119

**Draft Registration Card used during the September 12, 1918 Page 1**
**For men aged 18 through 45 as of June 5, 1918**

## REGISTRATION CARD

| SERIAL NUMBER | | | ORDER NUMBER | |
|---|---|---|---|---|

1

| First name | Middle name | Family Name |
|---|---|---|

**2 PERMANENT HOME ADDRESS**

| (No) | (Street or RFD Number) | (City or town) | (County) | (State) |
|---|---|---|---|---|

| 3. Age by Years | 4 Date of Birth | | |
|---|---|---|---|
| | (Month) | (Day) | (Year) |

### RACE

| | | | | Indian | |
|---|---|---|---|---|---|
| White | Negro | Oriental | Citizen | | Non-Citizen |
| 5 | 6 | 7 | 8 | | 9 |

| U.S. CITIZEN | | | ALIEN | |
|---|---|---|---|---|
| Native Born | Naturalized | Citizen by Father's Naturalization Before Registrant's Majority | Declarant | Non-Declarant |
| 10 | 11 | 12 | 13 | 14 |

15
If not a citizen of the U.S., of what nation are you a citizen or subject? _____

| PRESENT OCCUPATION | EMPLOYER'S NAME |
|---|---|
| 16 | 17 |

18  Place of Employment or Business

| (No) | (Street or RFD Number) | (City or town) | (County) | (State) |
|---|---|---|---|---|

| NEAREST RELATIVE | NAME | 19 | | | | |
|---|---|---|---|---|---|---|
| | ADDRESS | 20 | | | | |
| | | (No) | (Street or RFD Number) | (City or town) | (County) | (State) |

I AFFIRM THAT I HAVE VERIFIED ABOVE ANSWERS AND THAT THEY ARE TRUE.

P.M.G.O
Form No. 1          _____
                              Signature or Mark of Registrant

120

**Draft Registration Card used during the September 12, 1918**
**Registration – Page 2**

| REGISTRAR'S REPORT | | | | | | | |
|---|---|---|---|---|---|---|---|
| **DESCRIPTION OF REGISTRANT** | | | | | | | |
| **HEIGHT** | | | **BUILD** | | | **COLOR OF EYES** | **COLOR OF HAIR** |
| Tall | Medium | Short | Slender | Medium | Stout | | |
| 21 | 22 | 23 | 24 | 25 | 26 | 27 | 28 |

29  Has person lost arm, leg, hand, eye, or is he obviously physically disqualified?    (SPECIFY)

30  I certify that my answers are true, that the person registered has read or has had read to him his own answers, that I have witnessed his signature or mark and that all of his answers of which I have knowledge are true, except as follows:

———————————————————
Signature of Registrar

Date of Registration _____

(The stamp of the local board having jurisdiction of the area in which the registrant has his permanent home shall be placed in this box)

Taking them one at a time:

**National Archives**: All 24,000,000 of the draft registration cards have been microfilmed and are available by request from the National Archives, either by using NATF form 86 or ordering online at *eservices.archives.gov/orderonline*. The records are located at Microfilm list M1509, and the rolls are numbered according to state and county. You can go to *www.archives.gov/research/military/ww1/draft-registration/index.html* to see which roll a particular state and county is on. If none of the other options below have your ancestor's draft registration card available, try either the National Archives or the LDS Church.

**Ancestry.com**: Ancestry.com can also provide access to all 24,000,000 draft registration cards online. From the Ancestry.com home page, click on *Search* and select *Military* from the drop-down box. On the next page, in the middle of the *Browse Records* column, look for the *Military* label. As of this writing, *World War I draft registration cards* is the first entry. If it disappears by the time you go to look for it, simply click on *More*, and you will be able to locate it in the alphabetical list provided on the left-hand side of the page. It's one of the more frequently sought-after military records, so I suspect it will remain pretty easy to find. Or, if you wish, just go this URL: *search.ancestry.com/search/db.aspx?dbid=6482*.

**Other pay-for-service genealogy services**: As of this writing, Fold3 provides a few draft registration cards – about 5,000 at last count – a tiny percentage of those available, but they are adding records and collections all the time. If you have a Fold3 subscription, check it out. If not, you want to check Ancestry's collection.

Ancestry.com is available for free at most public libraries and the LDS Church's Family History Centers.

**Family History Library of the LDS Church**: The Family History Library of the LDS Church has microfilmed all 24,000,000 draft cards. So you can go to Salt Lake City, Utah to see them, or order them through your local Family History Center and view them locally. However, to do that, you'll need to know what state and county your ancestor lived in and registered for the draft.

**Other free locations:** There are several states, counties, genealogy societies and individuals who have taken it upon themselves to microfilm the draft cards for their jurisdiction or area of interest. Some of these collections are available online, while others are available at various state libraries in their genealogy collections, and may or may not be available through inter-library loan. Just Google *World War I draft registration cards (name of state where your ancestor lived in 1915)* for the most up-to-date listing of available sources.

## World War II records

As we get into the World War II era, we run into government privacy laws that protect personal information newer than 75 years, including military records. However, as discussed earlier, veterans and their next of kin can get access to their own personal military records.

But there is a set of military records from the World War II era that are available and of great value to researchers. They are World War II draft registration cards. In April 1942 the federal government required all men born between 28 September 1877 and 16 February 1897 (ages 45 to 64) to complete draft registration cards. The title used for these records is a bit misleading — the government wasn't interested in drafting these old guys, but instead was gleaning information on the industrial skills and capacity of these men. They wouldn't be used for military service, but the information provided the government with an inventory of the manpower resources available at that time. Apparently the resources weren't sufficient to meet our war-time manufacturing needs – remember Rosie the Riveter? Over 10,000,000 men completed these draft registration cards, and they are available, many of them online.

This registration, known as the *fourth registration*, or the *old man's registration*, the information available on the draft registration cards includes the following:

• Name
• Age
• Birth date
• Birth place

- Current residence
- Employer information
- Name and address of someone who would always know the whereabouts of the registrant
- Physical description of registrant (race, height, weight, eye and hair colors, complexion)

As you can see, good information about these men can be gleaned from these draft registration cards, just like those from World War I.

The database is unfortunately incomplete. In a (relatively) modern day tragedy, records from the following states were destroyed before they could be microfilmed – they are gone forever:

Alabama
Florida
Georgia
Kentucky
Mississippi
North Carolina
South Carolina
Tennessee

World War II draft registrations records provide genealogical information.

The information from these states represented approximately 10% of the records collected.

For the rest of the draft registration cards – still a massive number – the microfilmed records are available at the National Archives and can be ordered using NATF form 86, or by ordering online at *eservices.archives.gov/orderonline*. They are also available at the Family History Library, either to be viewed in Salt Lake City or to be borrowed and viewed at a local Family History Center at a local LDS church building.

Many of the records have also been digitized by Ancestry.com, and can be viewed with a subscription. As of this writing, the states they have digitized are:

Arkansas*
California*
Connecticut
Delaware
Illinois
Indiana*
Maryland
Massachusetts
New Hampshire
New Jersey
New York*
Ohio*
Pennsylvania
Puerto Rico
Rhode Island
Vermont
Virginia
West Virginia

* — the collections in the states marked with an asterisk are incomplete. In New York, cards from the five boroughs of New York City are all that exist.

The following pages contain templates for the World War II draft registration cards. As with the World War I cards, you can either copy these pages or e-mail me to get a copy. If you would like to get these online, you can download them from our website at *www.essentialgenealogy.com/forms__records.*

In addition to World War II draft registration cards, another source of great genealogical information is available from the World War II enlistment records – a collection that contains the names and information about all those who enlisted in any of the branches of the armed forces between 1938 and 1946. This collection

## World War II Draft Registration Card – Fourth registration – Page 1

**REGISTRATION CARD** – (Men born between April 28, 1877 and or before February 16, 1897)

| Serial Number<br>U_____ | 1. Name (Print)<br>_____<br>(First)      (Middle)      (Last) | Order<br>Number<br>_____ |
|---|---|---|

2. Place of Residence (Print)

_____

(Number and street)    (Town, township, village or city)    (State)

(THE PLACE OF RESIDENCE GIVEN ON THE LINE ABOVE WILL DETERMINE LOCAL BOARD JURISDICTION; LINE 2 OF REGISTRATION CERTIFICATE WILL BE IDENTICAL)
3. Mailing Address

_____

(Mailing address if other than place indicated on Line 2. If same, insert word *same*)

| 4. Telephone<br>_____<br>_____<br>(Exchange)  (Number) | 5. Age in Years<br>_____<br>Date of Birth<br>_____<br>(Mo)  (Day)  (Yr.) | 6. Place of Birth<br>_____<br>(Town or Country)<br>_____<br>(State or Country) |
|---|---|---|

7. Name and address of person who will always know your address

_____

8. Employer's name and address.

_____

9. Place of Employment or Business.

_____

(Number and street or RFD number)  (Town)  (County)  (State)

I AFFIRM THAT I HAVE VERIFIED ABOVE ANSWERS AND THAT THEY ARE TRUE.

D. S. S. Form 1

_____

(Revised 4-1-42)    (over)
(Registrant signature)

**World War II Draft Registration Card – Fourth registration – Page 2**

## REGISTRAR'S REPORT

| DESCRIPTION OF REGISTRANT | | | | | | | |
|---|---|---|---|---|---|---|---|
| **RACE** | | **HEIGHT** (Approx) | | **WEIGHT** (Approx) | | **COMPLEXION** | |
| White | | **EYES** | | **HAIR** | | Sallow | |
| Negro | | Blue | | Blonde | | Light | |
| Oriental | | Gray | | Red | | Ruddy | |
| Indian | | Hazel | | Brown | | Dark | |
| Filipino | | Brown | | Black | | Freckled | |
| | | Black | | Gray | | Light brown | |
| | | | | Bald | | Dark brown | |
| | | | | | | Black | |

Other obvious physical characteristics that will aid in identification _____
_____

I certify that my answers are true; that the person registered has read or has had read to him his own answers; that I have witnessed his signature or mark and that all of his answers of which I have knowledge are true, except as
follows:_____
_____

_____
Signature of Registrar)

Registrar for Local Board _____
                    (City or County)           (State)

Date of Registration _____

(The stamp of the Local Board having jurisdiction of
the registrant shall be placed in the above space)

can be found on the NARA website at *http://aad.archives.gov/aad/series-list.jsp?cat=WR26*. These records have been compiled (transcribed) on the NARA website. Check out the wonderful genealogical information available on these records:

- Name
- Residence (state and county)
- Date of enlistment
- Rank
- Branch
- Term of enlistment
- Nativity (state or country of birth)
- Year of birth
- Race and citizenship
- Education
- Civilian occupation
- Marital status
- Box and film reel number

A great find and a wonderful peek into history, not to mention genealogical information to assist you in your research.

### Other Resources for Military Records

As you begin to plow the fertile ground of military records in search of your ancestors, understand that that there are far more records available than I can possibly list in this book, or in several books. Veterans' census records, indexes to old soldiers' homes, indexes for soldiers' cemeteries, and veterans' societies are just a few of the other resources that are available. The Church of Jesus Christ of Latter-day Saints has published a sixty-page research outline for military records that gives an excellent overview of the records that are available to researchers: *United States Military Records*, Intellectual Reserve, Inc. It is available through the LDS Church Distribution Center in Salt Lake City, Utah (Tel. 800/537-5950) for a small fee. Or you can view and/or print it online by going to *www.familysearch.org*, selecting *Learn*, and then searching for it alphabetically. Or just go to this URL: *https://wiki.familysearch.org/en/United_States_Military_Records*. It is an excellent document.

**Korean War**

The Korean War (*conflict*) was fought between 1950 and 1954. Most miliary records from this war are not available. However, there are a number of websites available that list the US casualties of the Korean War, which were approximately 34,000, not including some 8,176 missing. Some of the websites also include another 100,000 or so that were wounded. Here are a couple of the websites that provide information on the US casualties:

- *search.ancestry.com/search/db.aspx?dbid=1033*
- *www.findmypast.com/articles/world-records/full-list-of-united-states-records/military-service-and-conflict/korean-war-deaths-1950-1954*
- *www.archives.gov/research/military/korean-war/casualty-lists/state-level-alpha.html,* (This website lists the casualties by home state.)
- *korea50.army.mil/features/casualties/index.shtml*

The records typically provide the service man's name, rank, branch of service, state of residence, birth, and death or injury dates.

**Vietnam War**

One of the most unpopular wars in United States history has a number of websites dedicated to it, and you can find information about those who gave their lives during the conflict. Over 58,000 US lives were lost in Vietnam. The floolowing website provide you information about these individuals:

- *www.findmypast.com/articles/world-records/full-list-of-united-states-records/military-service-and-conflict/vietnam-war-deaths*
- *www.archives.gov/research/military/vietnam-war/casualty-lists/co-alpha.pdf.* (This website lists the casualties by home state.)
- *search.ancestry.com/search/db.aspx?dbid=8846*
- *www.accessgenealogy.com/military/vietnam.php*

There is also an outstanding website featuring the Vietnam Mar Memorial in Washington, DC. It can be found at *http://thewall-usa.com/*. You'll find details about the war, the fallen, and a lot of interesting information about the conflict.

A link on the wall website also takes you to the records of fallen service men. As with the Korean War records, these records typically provide the service man's name, rank, branch of service, state of residence, birth, and death or injury dates.

FamilySearch.org has a tutorial on finding Vietnam War records at *https:// www.familysearch.org/learn/wiki/en/United_States_Vietnam_War_1964_to_1972.* In includes lists of records that are available, as well as links to a number of sources that provide casualty information.

# 11. SUMMARY

Well, that's it. Thanks for coming along on the ride with me. Over the course of a few pages we have discussed a number of resources – particularly those found in censuses and military records – that will hopefully assist you in finding your ancestors.

For me, in addition to providing me with great gobs of genealogical information, censuses also help my ancestors come alive for me. I see them gathered in a family setting, with father and mother and all their children clustered around them. Sometimes, grandma and grandpa are nearby – perhaps in the same home, or living on the farm next door. Often, the siblings and nieces and nephews of my ancestors are living nearby also.

I have a deep reverence for the military, and for those who stepped in harm's way to buy for us the freedoms we have today. Researching military records always leaves me with a sense of awe and not a little excitement when I find those whom I am seeking.

In these few pages I have shared some of my thoughts, tricks, and warnings about researching these two great sources of information. I hope it has been worth your time and effort, and I hope along the way you have uncovered some previously hidden ancestors.

If you've done much genealogy before, you know it can be a thrilling ride. In fact, that brings to mind a quote by Jenkin Lloyd Jones. He was describing a familial relationship – marriage – so I think it applicable to genealogy work. His first word was *Life*…I have changed it to *Doing genealogy:*

Doing genealogy is like an old-time rail journey – delays, sidetracks, smoke, dust, cinders, and jolts, interspersed occasionally by beautiful vistas and thrilling bursts of speed. The trick is to thank the Lord for letting you have the ride.

For those of you who are experienced genealogists – I suspect you are nodding right now and understand well his message. For those of you who are just beginning your journey – welcome aboard – and enjoy the journey!

# 12. GLOSSARY

**Agricultural census** – many states conducted agricultural censuses periodically. Generally just the head of household was named, along with acres owned, worked, planted in which types of grain, livestock, out buildings, etc. Agricultural censuses are generally of limited genealogical value, although they may aid in locating families at a certain time in a certain place.

**Census indexes** – census indexes have been developed for all the US and many of the state censuses, listing each person in the census. Errors in transcription of names by indexers, misspellings by enumerators, etc., may render some indexes frustrating to use. Generally speaking, however, they are a great aid to researchers. However, depending entirely upon them may cause researchers to miss families whose names were misspelled, either in the index or on the census itself.

**Compiled Military Service Records (CMSRs)** – CMSRs were records kept for the Union and Confederate soldiers and officers. Each soldier will have one for each regiment in which he served. Information found in CMSRs includes biographical and medical information, physical description, pay vouchers, marital status and other personal information like leave requests and commendations. CMSRs were not kept for regular Army soldiers and officers.

**City directories** – some city telephone directories in the latter part of the 19th and early 20th centuries provide researchers with another way to locate families in a given place at a given time.

**Date formats** – an important aspect of genealogical research is consistency in date formats so as not to confuse months and days. The standard format is DD/MON/

YYYY, with the month either abbreviated with three letters, or spelled out, and the year always given as four digits: 24 APR 1882.

**Enumeration district** – the area a particular census covers. Typically a county or township or town. Larger towns and cities are divided into multiple Enumeration Districts.

**Enumerators** – those wonderful souls who accepted employment to tabulate the population of the United States. Enumerators employed their craft every ten years since 1790. Genealogists owe a great deal to these intrepid census workers.

**Fold3** – formerly Footnote.com, a subscription genealogy service. After Footnote's purchase by Ancestry.com, its name was changed to Fold3; the new name is derived from the third fold in a traditional military flag folding ceremony which "is made in honor and remembrance of the veteran departing our ranks who gave a portion of his or her life for the defense of our country to attain peace throughout the world." An appropriate name for a genealogy service that focuses on military records.

**Genealogy societies** – groups of like-minded individuals who band together to do genealogical research. Societies may focus on a geographic area, ethnic research, surname research, etc.

**Immigration records** – any of various government records produced at the time an individual immigrates to or emigrates from a location. Included are ships passenger lists, oaths of allegiance, etc. Immigration records are often filled with genealogical information.

**Indian census rolls** – special censuses of Indians were undertaken between 1885 and 1940 as part of the US census enumeration. The Indian census rolls are separate schedules from the regular census, and provide genealogical information on Indian ancestors.

**Industrial censuses** — many states conducted industrial censuses periodically. Generally just the head of household was named, along with his/her business, machinery owned, goods produced, etc. Industrial censuses are generally of limited genealogical value, although they may aid in locating families at a certain time in a certain place.

**Mortality schedules** – during the 1850 through 1880 censuses, a special schedule was completed that listed the names of all individuals who had died in the year previous to the census. Information on their name, age, sex, illness, duration of illness, etc., was captured. Each of these individuals is tied to a family in the regular census. This is an often-overlooked source of genealogical information.

**National Archives** – abbreviated as NARA, the National Archives are the repository of all the nation's records – censuses, military, passport, immigration and naturalization, etc. A vast storehouse of information, copies of records can be ordered, viewed in Washington DC or possibly in one of fourteen regional National Archive facilities. Many of the records currently held by NARA are finding their way online through the efforts of NARA as well as subscription services like Ancestry.com and Fold3.

**Naturalization records** — any of various government records produced at the time an individual immigrates to or emigrates from a location. Included are requests for citizenship (aka citzenship petitions). Naturalization records are often filled with genealogical information.

**Research plan** – a plan set down by a genealogist before s/he begins researching an ancestor. Included is relevant information – the ancestor's name, spouse's name, maiden name of women, likely places where information may be found, and the information being sought. Research plans assist genealogists in focusing their research.

**Slave schedules** – Separate slave schedules were enumerated during the 1850 and 1860 censuses. Prior to that, slaves were included in the tally of the slave owner's family. In the 1850 and 1860 slave schedules, slaves are listed under the slave owner's name, but a notation indicates whether they were in the employ of another individual. These listings provide only the slave owner's name and the name of the individual who rented the slave from the owner – the slave's name is not included. In the deep south, some plantations listed the names of each slave. Slaves over 100 years old were listed by name in the 1850 and 1860 slave schedules.

**Special interim census** — the special interim census of 1885 was funded by the federal government for a handful of states: Colorado, Florida, Nebraska and North and South Dakota territories as well as New Mexico Territory. It asked essentially the same questions as the 1880 census used for the rest of the United States. It is of particular value since the 1890 census was lost.

**Territorial censuses** – before they became states, a number of territories also had censuses taken. The questions were the same as those on the census for the states.

**Veterans' schedules** – special schedules for veterans were included in the 1840 and 1890 federal censuses. They identified by name those veterans of the Revolutionary War and War of 1812 (1840) and veterans of the Civil War and Mexican Wars (1890).

# APPENDICES

## APPENDIX A: QUESTIONS ASKED IN THE UNITED STATES CENSUSES

**1790 — Enumeration date 2 August 1790**
• Head of family
• Free White Males
• 16 and up, including head of family
• Under 16
• Free white females
• Including head
• All other persons
• Slaves
• County
• City

Note: No schedules are known to exist for the 1790 Census for Delaware, Georgia, Kentucky, New Jersey, Tennessee, and Virginia. It is thought that they were destroyed during the War of 1812 when the British attacked Washington. Some Virginia records are available from state enumeration records taken in 1790.

**1800 — Enumeration date 4 August 1800**
• Head of family
• Free white males
• Under 10
• 10 to 16
• 16 to 26
• 26 to 45
• 45 and over
• Free white females
• Under 10
• 10 to 16
• 16 to 26
• 26 to 45
• 45 and over
• All others
• Slaves
• Remarks

**1810 — Enumeration date 6 August 1810**
(Same as 1800)

**1820 — Enumeration date 7 August 1820**
• Head of family
• Free white males
• Under 10
• 10 to 16
• 16 to 18
• 16 to 26
• 26 to 45
• 45 and over
• Free white females
• Under 10
• 10 to 16
• 16 to 18
• 16 to 26
• 26 to 45
• 45 and over
• Foreigners not naturalized
• Agriculture
• Commerce
• Manufacturers
• Free coloreds
• Slaves
• Remarks

**1830 — Enumeration date 1 June 1830**
• Head of family
• Free white males
• Under 5, 5 to 10, 10 to 15, 15 to 20, 20 to 30, 30 to 40, 40 to 50, 50 to 60, 60 to 70, 70 to 80, 80 to 90, 90 to 100, over 100
• Free white females
• Under 5, 5 to 10, 10 to 15, 15 to 20, 20 to 30, 30 to 40, 40 to 50, 50 to 60, 60 to 70, 70 to 80, 80 to 90, 90 to 100, over 100
• Slaves
• Free colored

**1840 – Enumeration Date 1 June 1840**
(Same as 1830)

**1850 – Enumeration Date 1 June 1850**
• Name

- Age
- Sex
- Color
- Occupation
- Value of real estate
- Birthplace
- Married within year
- School within year
- Cannot read or write
- Enumeration date
- Remarks

## 1860 – Enumeration Date 1 June 1860
- Name
- Age
- Sex
- Color
- Occupation
- Value of real estate
- Value of personal property
- Birthplace
- Married in year
- School in year
- Cannot read or write
- Enumeration date
- Remarks

## 1870 – Enumeration date 1 June 1870
- Name
- Age
- Sex
- Color
- Occupation
- Value of real estate
- Value of personal property
- Birthplace
- Father foreign born
- Mother foreign born
- Month born in census year
- School in census year
- Can't read or write
- Eligible to vote
- Date of enumeration

**1880 — Enumeration date 1 June 1880**
- Name
- Color
- Sex
- Age June 1 in census year
- Relationship to head of house
- Single
- Married
- Widowed
- Divorced
- Married in census year
- Occupation
- Other information
- Can't read or write
- Place of birth
- Place of birth of father
- Place of birth of mother
- Enumeration date

**1890 — Enumeration date 1 June 1890**
Note: Tragically, the vast majority of the 1890 Census was destroyed in a fire (or by the water that was used to put out the fire!). A few census records survived, and a number of parties have cobbled together information about the 1890 population through various Indian Territory schedules, city directories, 1890 veteran schedules, etc.

**1900 — Enumeration date 1 June 1900**
- Name of each person whose place of abode on June 1, 1900 was in this family
- Relation to head of family
- Sex
- Color
- Month of birth
- Year of birth
- Age
- Marital status
- Number of years married
- Mother of how many children
- Number of these children living
- Place of birth
- Place of birth of father
- Place of birth of mother
- Years of immigration to US
- Number of years in US

- Naturalization
- Occupation
- Number of months not employed
- Attended school (months)
- Can read
- Can write
- Can speak English
- Home owned or rented
- Home owned free or mortgaged
- Farm or house

**Note** that the 1900 US census asks for the month and year of birth. This may be very helpful in identifying a primary source (like a birth certificate) for this person.

### 1910 — Enumeration date 15 April 1910
- Name of each person whose place of abode on April 15, 1910 was in this family
- Relation to head of family
- Sex
- Race
- Age
- Marital status
- Number of years married
- Mother of how many children
- Number of these children living
- Place of birth
- Place of birth of father
- Place of birth of mother
- Years of immigration to US
- Naturalized or alien
- Language spoken
- Occupation
- Nature of trade
- Employer, worker or own account
- Number of months not employed
- Can read and write
- Attending school
- Home owned or rented
- Home owned free or mortgaged
- Farm or house
- Whether a survivor of the Union or Confederate Army or Navy
- Blind or deaf-mute

**1920 — Enumeration date 1 January 1920**
- Name of each person whose place of abode on January 1, 1920 was in this family
- Relation to head of family
- Home owned or rented
- Home owned free or mortgaged
- Sex
- Color or race
- Age
- Marital status
- Years of immigration to US
- Naturalized or alien
- Year of naturalization
- Attending school
- Can read or write
- Place of birth
- Mother tongue
- Place of birth of father
- Mother tongue of father
- Place of birth of mother
- Mother tongue of mother
- Can speak English
- Occupation

**1930 — Enumeration date 1 April 1930**
- Name of each person whose place of abode on April 1, 1930 was in this family
- Relationship of this person to the head of the family
- Home owned or rented
- Value of home, if owned, or monthly rental, if rented
- Radio set
- Does this family own a farm?
- Color or race
- Age at last birthday
- Marital condition
- Age at first marriage
- Attended school or college any time since Sept. 1, 1929
- Whether able to read or write
- Place of birth
- Place of birth of father
- Place of birth of mother
- Mother tongue (or native language) of foreign born
- Year of immigration into the United States
- Naturalization
- Whether able to speak English

- Trade, profession, or particular kind of work done
- Industry or business
- Class of worker
- Whether actually at work yesterday
- Whether a veteran of U.S. Military or naval forces
- What war or expedition
- Number of farm schedule

**1940 — Enumeration date 1 April 1940**
- Address (number and street)
- Name of each person whose place of abode on April 1, 1930 was in this family
- Relationship of this person to the head of the family
- Home owned or rented
- Value of home, if owned, or monthly rental, if rented
- Radio set
- Does this household live on a farm?
- Color or race
- Age at last birthday
- Marital condition
- Age at first marriage
- Attended school or college any time since March 1, 1940
- Highest grade of school completed
- Whether able to read or write
- Place of birth
- Citizenship of the foreign born
- Whether a veteran of U.S. Military or naval forces
- Whether wife, widow or under-18-year-old child of a veteran
- Veterans – war or military service
- Residence on April 1, 1935
- Employment status (ten questions on employment status)
- Income in 1939
- Place of birth of father
- Place of birth of mother
- Mother tongue (or native language) of foreign born
- Usual occupation
- Usual industry
- Income earned in 1939
- For all women who are or have been married:
- Has this woman been married more than once
- Age at first marriage
- Number of children ever born (do not include stillbirths)
- Number of farm schedule

## APPENDIX B: A SYNOPSIS OF MORTALITY SCHEDULES BY STATE

**Alabama** — Mortality schedules exist for the 1850, 1860, 1870, and 1880 censuses.

**Alaska** — Mortality schedules do not exist for Alaska.

**Arizona** — Mortality schedules exist for the 1850, 1860, 1870, and 1880 censuses.

**Arkansas** — Mortality schedules exist for the 1870 and 1880 censuses.

**California** — Mortality schedules exist for the 1850, 1860, 1870, and 1880 censuses.

**Colorado** — Mortality schedules exist for the 1860, 1870, and 1880 censuses. There is also a mortality schedule associated with a special interim census conducted in Colorado in 1885.

**Connecticut** — Mortality schedules exist for the 1850, 1860, 1870, and 1880 censuses.

**Delaware** — Mortality schedules exist for the 1850, 1860, 1870, and 1880 censuses.

**District of Columbia** — Mortality schedules exist for the 1850, 1860, 1870, and 1880 censuses.

**Florida** — Mortality schedules exist for the 1850, 1860, 1870, and 1880 censuses. There is also a mortality schedule associated with a special interim census conducted in Florida in 1885.

**Georgia** — Mortality schedules exist for the 1850, 1860, 1870, and 1880 censuses.

**Hawaii** — There are no mortality schedules available for Hawaii.

**Idaho** — Mortality schedules exist for the 1870 and 1880 censuses.

**Illinois** — Mortality schedules exist for the 1850, 1860, 1870, and 1880 censuses.

**Indiana** — Mortality schedules exist for the 1850, 1860, 1870, and 1880 censuses.

**Iowa** — Mortality schedules exist for the 1850, 1860, 1870, and 1880 censuses.

**Kansas** — Mortality schedules exist for the 1860, 1870, and 1880 censuses.

**Kentucky** — Mortality schedules exist for the 1850, 1860, 1870, and 1880 censuses.

**Louisiana** — Mortality schedules exist for the 1850, 1860, 1870, and 1880 censuses.

**Maine** — Mortality schedules exist for the 1850, 1860, 1870, and 1880 censuses.

**Maryland** — Mortality schedules exist for the 1850, 1860, 1870, and 1880 censuses.

**Massachusetts** — Mortality schedules exist for the 1850, 1860, 1870, and 1880 censuses.

**Michigan** — Mortality schedules exist for the 1850, 1860, 1870, and 1880 censuses.

**Minnesota** — Mortality schedules exist for the 1850, 1860 and 1870censuses.

**Mississippi** — Mortality schedules exist for the 1850, 1860, 1870, and 1880 censuses.

**Missouri** — Mortality schedules exist for the 1850, 1860, 1870, and 1880 censuses.

**Montana** — Mortality schedules exist for the 1860 and 1870 censuses.

**Nebraska** — Mortality schedules exist for the 1860, 1870, and 1880 censuses. There is also a mortality schedule associated with a special interim census conducted in 1885.

**Nevada** — Mortality schedules exist for the 1860 and 1870 censuses.

**New Hampshire** — Mortality schedules exist for the 1850, 1860, 1870, and 1880 censuses.

**New Jersey** — Mortality schedules exist for the 1850, 1860, 1870, and 1880 censuses.

**New Mexico** — Mortality schedules exist for the 1850, 1860, and 1870 censuses. There is also a mortality schedule associated with a special interim census conducted in New Mexico in 1885.

**New York** — Mortality schedules exist for the 1850, 1860, 1870, and 1880 censuses.

**North Carolina** — Mortality schedules exist for the 1850, 1860, 1870, and 1880 censuses. There is also a mortality schedule associated with a special interim census conducted in North Carolina in 1885.

**North Dakota** — Mortality schedules exist for the 1860, 1870 and 1880 censuses. There is also a mortality schedule associated with a special interim census conducted in North Dakota in 1885.

**Ohio** — Mortality schedules exist for the 1850, 1860 and 1880 censuses.

**Oklahoma** — Oklahoma had no mortality schedules.

**Oregon** — Mortality schedules exist for the 1850, 1860, 1870, and 1880 censuses.

**Pennsylvania** — Mortality schedules exist for the 1850, 1860, 1870, and 1880 censuses.

**Rhode Island** — Mortality schedules exist for the 1850, 1860, 1870, and 1880 censuses.

**South Carolina** — Mortality schedules exist for the 1870 census.

**South Dakota** — Mortality schedules exist for the 1860, 1870, and 1880 censuses. There is also a mortality schedule associated with a special interim census conducted in South Dakota in 1885.

**Tennessee** — Mortality schedules exist for the 1850, 1860,1870, and 1880 censuses.

**Texas** — Mortality schedules exist for the 1850, 1860, 1870, and 1880 censuses.

**Utah** — Mortality schedules exist for the 1850, 1860, 1870, and 1880 censuses.

**Vermont** — Mortality schedules exist for the 1850, 1860, 1870, and 1880 censuses.

**Virginia** — Mortality schedules exist for the 1850, 1860, 1870, and 1880 censuses.

**Washington** — Mortality schedules exist for the 1860, 1870, and 1880 censuses.

**West Virginia** — Mortality schedules exist for the 1850, 1860, 1870, and 1880 censuses.

**Wisconsin** — Mortality schedules exist for the 1850, 1860, 1870, and 1880 censuses.

**Wyoming** — Mortality schedules exist for the 1870 and 1880 censuses.

# INDEX

# GENEALOGICAL NOTES

# GENEALOGICAL NOTES